Private Client Investment Advice and Management (PCIAM)

The Official Learning and Reference Manual

Covering the following modules:

Module 1: Financial Advice within a Regulated Environment

Module 2: Investment Taxation

Module 3: Financial Markets

Module 4: Trust and Trustees

1st Edition, Revised September 2013
Volume I

PROFESSIONALISM | INTEGRITY | EXCELLENCE

Private Client Investment Advice and Management

Welcome to the Chartered Institute for Securities & Investment's *Private Client Investment Advice and Management (PCIAM)* study material.

This workbook has been written to prepare you for the Chartered Institute for Securities & Investment's *Private Client Investment Advice and Management (PCIAM)* examination.

PUBLISHED BY:

Chartered Institute for Securities & Investment
© Chartered Institute for Securities & Investment 2013
8 Eastcheap
London
EC3M IAE
Tel: +44 (0) 20 7645 0600
Fax: + 44 (0) 20 7645 0601

WRITTEN BY:

David Coard

Derek Huish

REVIEWED BY:

A R Hales TD, Chartered FCSI

This is an educational manual only and Chartered Institute for Securities & Investment accepts no responsibility for persons undertaking trading or investments in whatever form.

While every effort has been made to ensure its accuracy, no responsibility for loss occasioned to any person acting or refraining from action as a result of any material in this publication can be accepted by the publisher or authors.

A Learning Map, which contains the full syllabus, appears at the end of this workbook. The syllabus can also be viewed on the Institute's website at cisi.org and is also available by contacting Customer Support on +44 20 7645 0777. Please note that the examination is based upon the syllabus. Candidates are reminded to check the Candidate Update area of the Institute's website (cisi.org) on a regular basis for updates that could affect their exam as a result of industry change.

The questions contained in this manual are designed as an aid to revision of different areas of the syllabus and to help you consolidate your learning chapter by chapter.

Workbook version: 1.3 (September 2013)

FOREWORD

Learning and Professional Development with the CISI

The Chartered Institute for Securities & Investment evolved from the London Stock Exchange and was initially known as the Securities Institute. We currently have around 50,000 members, who benefit from a programme of professional and social events, with continuing professional development (CPD) and the promotion of integrity very much at the heart of everything we do.

This learning manual (or 'workbook' as it is often known in the industry) provides not only a thorough preparation for the CISI examination it refers to, but is a valuable desktop reference for practitioners. It can also be used as a learning tool for readers interested in knowing more, but not necessarily entering an examination.

The CISI official learning manuals ensure that candidates gain a comprehensive understanding of examination content. Our material is written and updated by industry specialists and reviewed by experienced, senior figures in the financial services industry. Quality is assured through a rigorous editorial system of practitioner panels and boards. CISI examinations are used extensively by firms to meet the requirements of government regulators. The CISI works closely with a number of international regulators that recognise our examinations and the manuals supporting them, as well as the UK regulators, the Financial Conduct Authority (FCA). and the Prudential Regulation Authority (PRA).

CISI learning manuals are normally revised annually. It is important that candidates check they purchase the correct version for the period when they wish to take their examination. Between versions, candidates should keep abreast of the latest industry developments through the Candidate Update area of the CISI website, cisi.org/candidateupdate. (The CISI also accredits the manuals of certain Accredited Training Providers.)

The CISI produces a range of elearning revision tools such as Revision Express Interactive that can be used in conjunction with our learning and reference manuals. For further details, please visit cisi.org. The CISI is committed to using the latest technology to introduce interactivity in its revision tools, and, over time, the Revision Express Interactive will be expanded for each examination.

The questions in the manuals are selected to be at the same standard as the questions in the examination itself, but they are not the same questions as in the examination. During 2013, mock examination papers will be made available on our website, as an additional revision tool.

As a Professional Body, around 50,000 CISI members subscribe to the CISI Code of Conduct and the CISI has a significant voice in the industry, standing for professionalism, excellence and the promotion of trust and integrity. Continuing professional development is at the heart of the Institute's values. Our CPD scheme is available free of charge to members, and this includes an online record-keeping system as well as regular seminars, conferences and professional networks in specialist subject areas, all of which cover a range of current industry topics. Reading this manual and taking a CISI examination is credited as professional development with the CISI CPD scheme. To learn more about CISI membership, visit cisi.org/membership.

We hope that you will find this manual useful and interesting. Once you have completed it, you will find helpful suggestions on qualifications and membership progression with the CISI at the end of this book. We are also always pleased to receive comments and feedback; please see cisi.org/feedback.

With best wishes for your studies.

Ruth Martin
Managing Director

CONTENTS

MODULE ONE

FINANCIAL ADVICE WITHIN A REGULATED ENVIRONMENT

An exam specification breakdown is provided at the back of this workbook

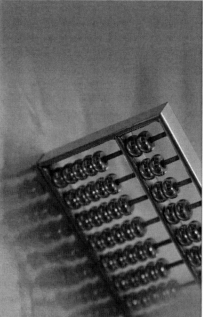

1. INTRODUCTION

In this module we will be building on your knowledge, looking in greater detail at the implications of the UK legal and regulatory framework and how this impacts on the provision of private client investment advice.

Some of the terminology and concepts will already be familiar to you in your day-to-day work. We will build upon this knowledge and seek to strengthen your ability to apply the knowledge to real life. We hope that this will give you confidence for your examination.

You must continue reading and extending your understanding around the topics covered through additional study. This workbook does not represent everything you may be expected to know for the examination.

You will see icons or symbols alongside the text. These indicate activities or questions that have been designed to check your understanding and help you validate your understanding.

Here is a guide as to what each of the symbols means:

 Question

This identifies a question that will enable you to check your knowledge and understanding.

 Analyse

This gives you an opportunity to consider a question posed and compare your answers to the feedback given.

 Test

At the end of the module, you will have the opportunity to validate your learning by attempting questions which require knowledge of these topics.

1.1   OBJECTIVES

1. Understand the main provisions of FSMA 2000 and associated secondary legislation, and assess their implications for the business operations of the private client adviser.

2. Understand the aims of the European Financial Services Action Plan, and evaluate the effects of MiFID and CRD on the business systems and controls of the private client adviser.

3. Understand the role, regulatory objectives and functions of the PRA and FCA and how they affect the control structures of firms.

4. Relate the FCA's Principles and Conduct of Business rules to the processes of advising clients, managing investments and reporting to customers.

5. Apply the rules on 'treating customers fairly' and 'client's best interest' to the process of advising clients.

6. Know the extent of an investment adviser's duty to disclose material information about a recommended investment.

7. Identify 'conflicts of interest' and their potential impact on clients and business operations and understand the compliance requirements that exist to prevent such occurrences.

8. Understand the fiduciary responsibilities of intermediaries, the rights of aggrieved customers and the rules for handling complaints.

9. Understand the principal measures to combat financial crime (insider dealing, market abuse, money laundering) and evaluate their impact on the firm, the private client adviser and the process of advising and managing client investments.

2. FSMA 2000 AND THE REGULATORY BODIES

2.1 REGULATORY FRAMEWORK

Up to 1986, the City and financial institutions had been mainly self-regulating. The ethos was *dictum meum pactum* ('my word is my bond'). However with the new Conservative government of 1979 ushering in a new era of home and share ownership to the general public, there was recognition that a more robust regulatory framework needed to be created. This would help protect those new shareholders.

The Government appointed Professor Gower to report, and a hybrid system of self-regulation within a statutory framework would be created through the Financial Services Act 1986. Through this act, firms would now be required to be authorised in order to conduct investment business.

When, in 1997, Labour came to power, the industry had seen several calamitous events, all of which undermined both the reputation of the City institutions and the individuals who worked within them. All were highly publicised and well known to the general public, many of whom had been using financial instruments to a greater or lesser degree.

These events included:

*   widespread pension mis-selling;
*   the collapse of Barings;
*   the Maxwell pension fraud.

The Chancellor announced a radical reform of the financial services industry, which included independence for the Bank of England, and the creation of a single statutory regulator. So the Financial Services and Markets Act 2000 (FSMA 2000) came into force on 30 November 2001 (a date we refer to as 'N2') and with the Act came the creation of the Financial Services Authority (FSA) in statute law, together with statutory powers, a single ombudsman and compensation scheme.

2.2 THE NEW REGULATORY STRUCTURE IN THE UK

After a consultation period, HM Treasury issued a document in February 2011 *'A New Approach to Financial Regulation: Building A Stronger System'*. This was enacted by the **Financial Services Act 2012**. The FSA was divided into two bodies:

*   **The Prudential Regulatory Authority (PRA)** – established (as an operationally independent subsidiary of the Bank of England) for regulation of deposit-takers (ie, banks), insurers, and systemically important investment firms.
*   **The Financial Conduct Authority (FCA)** – responsible for conduct issues across the entire spectrum of financial services; it is also be responsible for market supervision as well as the prudential supervision of firms not supervised by the PRA.

In addition, the **Financial Policy Committee (FPC)** was established in the Bank of England, charged with a primary objective of identifying, monitoring and taking action to remove or reduce systemic risks with a view to protecting and enhancing the resilience of the UK financial system. The FPC has a secondary objective to support the economic policy of the Government.

In early 2013, the FSA replaced its old risk and supervision business units with a prudential business unit and a conduct business unit (covering consumer and markets) in preparation for the move to the new regulatory structure – which took effect from 1 April 2013.

To ensure that the new regulatory structure would be in place as at 1 April 2013, the FSA moved to a **twin peaks** model – this meant that banks, building societies, insurers and major investment firms had two groups of supervisors: one focusing on prudential and one focusing on conduct. All other firms (ie, those not dual-regulated) were solely supervised by the conduct supervisors.

Simplified Picture of the New Regulatory Framework

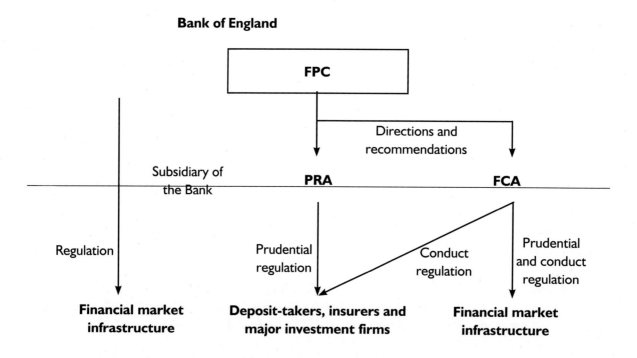

2.2.1 The Prudential Regulation Authority (PRA)

The PRA's role is to contribute to the promotion of the stability of the UK financial system through the micro-prudential regulation of the types of firms set out above. It will have an overall objective to promote the safety and soundness of regulated firms, and will meet this objective primarily by seeking to minimise any adverse effects of firm failure on the UK financial system and by ensuring that firms carry on their business in a way that avoids adverse effects on the system.

For insurance supervision, the PRA has two complementary objectives – to secure an appropriate degree of protection for policyholders and, as needed, to minimise the adverse impact that the failure of an insurer or the way it carries out its business could have on the stability of the system.

The PRA supervises around 1,000 deposit-takers, some 330 banks, 50 building societies and 600 credit unions as well as a number of investment banks that have the potential to present significant risk to the stability of the financial system.

2.2.2   The Financial Policy Committee (FPC)

The FPC is an official committee of the Bank of England. It focuses on the macro-economic and financial issues that may threaten the stability of the financial system and economic objectives including growth and employment.

It is charged with identifying, monitoring and taking action to reduce systemic risks with a view to protecting and enhancing the resilience of the UK financial system.

The FPC makes recommendations and gives directions to the PRA on specific actions that should be taken in order to achieve its objectives. The PRA is responsible for implementing FPC recommendations on a 'comply or explain' basis, and for complying with the FPC's directions in relation to the use of macro-prudential tools, specified by HM Treasury legislation. The PRA reports to the FPC on its delivery of these recommendations and directions.

The PRA provides firm-specific information to the FPC, to assist its macro-prudential supervision. The FPC's assessment of systemic risks influences the PRA's judgements in pursuit of its own judgement.

2.2.3   The Financial Conduct Authority (FCA)

The FCA's key aim is to ensure financial markets work well so consumers get a fair deal.

To do this, the FCA has a single strategic objective, to ensure that the relevant markets are functioning well. It also has three operational objectives, which are to:

- secure an appropriate degree of protection for consumers;
- protect and enhance the integrity of the financial system;
- promote effective competition in the interests of consumers.

Underlining the operational objectives are the following three broad outcomes:

- Consumers get financial services and products that meet their needs from firms they can trust.
- Firms compete effectively with the interests of their customers and the integrity of the market at the heart of how they run their business.
- Markets and financial systems are sound, stable and resilient with transparent pricing information.

The FCA kept the previous regulator's (the FSA) policy of credible deterrence, pursuing enforcement cases to punish wrongdoing. Its market regulation will continue to promote integrity and carry on the fight against insider dealing, in which the previous regulator secured 20 criminal convictions since 2009.

The FCA's approach to and style of supervision is different to that of the previous regulator (the FSA). The FCA carries out in-depth structured supervision work with those firms with the potential to cause the greatest risks to their objectives. This means fewer supervisors allocated to specific firms – but allows the FCA greater flexibility to carry out more reviews on products and issues across a particular sector or market thematic reviews. This new approach is underpinned by judgement-based supervisions.

The FCA's integrity objective includes within it the *soundness, stability and resilience* of the UK financial system. With regards to resilience, the FCA expects firms to operate high standards in their risk management, having procedures in place to ensure continuity of critical services. Firms are required to comply with standards for resilience and recovery set in this area.

To ensure that the relevant markets work well, the FCA has increased its focus on delivering good market conduct. The FCA's key priorities in delivering good market conduct are:

- a renewed focus on wholesale conduct – in particular inherent conflicts of interest;
- trust in the integrity of markets;
- preventing market abuse.

The National Audit Officer (NAO) is the statutory auditor of the FCA, with the power to carry out value-for-money reviews. HMT can also carry out economy, efficiency and effectiveness reviews.

2.3   REGULATED ACTIVITIES AND INVESTMENTS

Under General Prohibition of FSMA 2000, all firms undertaking a regulated activity must be authorised or exempt. Those exempt are:

- Bank of England/central banks/IMF etc.
- Local authorities/charities (deposits only).
- Appointed representatives.
- Recognised Investment Exchanges (RIEs).
- Recognised Clearing Houses (RCHs).

The list of regulated activities (Regulated Activities Order 2001) for which firms must be authorised (Part 4A Permissions) to transact business, has expanded since the original list was created, and now covers the following:

- Dealing in investments as principal or agent.
- Arranging deals in investments.
- Managing investments.
- Advising on investments.
- Providing basic advice on stakeholder products.
- Establishing operating or winding up a collective investment scheme.
- Establishing operating or winding up a pension scheme.
- Sending dematerialised instructions in investments.
- Safeguarding and administering investments.
- Accepting deposits.
- Issuing e-money.
- Funeral plan providers;.
- Lloyds – advice on syndicate participation or managing the underwriting of syndicates;.
- Mortgage-related activities.
- Home reversion and home finance activities.
- Effecting and carrying out contracts of insurance and insurance mediation.
- Operating a Multilateral Trading Facility (MTF).

To be clear, the Act also outlines the specified investments within these activities that cover:

- Shares.
- Bonds and other forms of indebtedness, eg, CDs.
- Certificates representing investments, eg, ADRs or GDRs;.
- Instruments giving entitlements, eg, warrants.
- Units in a collective investment scheme.
- Options.
- Futures (excluding those agreed for commercial purposes as opposed to investment/speculative purposes).
- Contracts for difference.
- Rights under a stakeholder pension scheme.
- Deposits.
- Long-term insurance (life).
- General insurance.
- Lloyds syndicate capacity and membership.
- Funeral plan contracts.
- Regulated mortgage contracts.
- Home reversion plans and home purchase plans eg, equity release schemes.
- Electronic monies.

As advising on and managing investments is covered, we should remember that it is a **criminal offence** to carry on investment business in the UK without authorisation, which carries a maximum two-year jail term and/or unlimited fine. Also an **unauthorised firm** cannot enforce an investment agreement and will have to make good any losses to clients and/or pay any profit from contracts entered into when unauthorised.

2.4 STATUS AND STRUCTURE OF THE FCA

The FCA is a private company limited by guarantee, which is owned by the Government and wholly financed by the financial services industry via a fee structure.

The FCA is accountable to the Treasury, to which it submits an annual report, and through an Annual General Meeting where the general public, as well as the industry, are invited to review its activities. The FCA is accountable to the Treasury through a variety of mechanisms. The Treasury has the power to appoint or dismiss the FCA's board and chairman. The FCA must carry out an investigation and report to HM Treasury if there has been a significant regulatory failure.

The Treasury has the power to commission reviews and inquiries into aspects of the FCA's operations. Reviews are to be conducted by someone whom the Treasury feels is independent of the FCA, and are restricted to considering the economy, efficiency and effectiveness with which the FCA has used its resources in discharging its functions. Such inquiries may relate to specific, exceptional events occurring within the FCA's range of regulatory responsibilities.

2.4.1 Objectives of the FCA

In July 2013 the FCA published a document titled *The FCA's Approach to Advancing its Objectives*. The paper was guidance on how the FCA would approach its statutory objectives, as well as requesting for comments on their approach.

The main purpose of the guidance document was to show how they intend to meet their three operational objectives and explain what firms and consumers can expect from the FCA.

The FCA has three main operational objectives covering protecting consumers; market integrity and promoting effective competition.

Protecting Consumers

The FCA explains in their **consumer protection objective**, how they will secure an appropriate degree of protection for consumers, and what this means to the businesses and markets that they regulate.

Therefore, the FCA aims to:

- ensure customers are treated in a way that is appropriate for their level of financial knowledge and understanding;
- be more outward looking, by engaging more with consumers and understanding more about their concerns and behaviour;
- set clear expectations for firms and be clear about what firms can expect from them;
- intervene early to tackle potential risks to consumers before they take shape;
- be tougher and bolder, following a strategy of credible deterrence, using new powers of intervention and enforcement.

The FCA have a competition duty to promote effective competition when addressing the consumer protection (or market integrity) objective. What the competition duty means is that they will look to achieve the desired outcomes using solutions that promote competition regardless of which objective they are pursuing.

The FCA will normally choose the most pro-competitive measure that is compatible with their duties as a whole. Consideration of how to apply this in practice will be made on a case-by-case basis.

Market Integrity

The FCA's **market integrity objective** is to protect and enhance the integrity of the UK financial system, they are concerned with a number of things, including:

- the soundness, stability and resilience of the financial markets;
- the transparency of the price information process in those markets;
- combating market abuse;
- the orderly operation of the financial markets;
- reducing financial crime in the UK financial system.

They also have a competition duty to promote effective competition when addressing the market integrity (or consumer protection) objective. What the competition duty means is that the FCA will look to achieve the desired outcomes using solutions that promote competition regardless of which objective they are pursuing.

To ensure that the relevant markets work well, the FCA has stated that they will focus on delivering good market conduct. They will intervene pro-actively to make markets more efficient and resilient, improving integrity and choice.

The FCA aims to ensure that market infrastructure is sound and well-run, so that users of markets have confidence in the reliability of the pricing processes and are confident that the transactions they enter into are properly executed. To perform this role, the FCA will look at a wide range of behaviour that damages trust in the integrity of markets or threatens consumer protection.

In their supervision of markets the FCA will look at wholesale conduct, for example, looking at and getting involved where they see poor behaviour by the parties concerned that have a wider impact on trust in the integrity of markets, or where inappropriate activity is likely to have poor consequences for retail consumers.

Promoting Effective Competition

The FCA has a **competition objective** to promote effective competition in the interests of consumers in the markets they regulate. They also have a competition duty to promote effective competition when addressing the consumer protection or market integrity objectives.

What the competition duty means is that they will look to achieve the desired outcomes using solutions that promote competition regardless of the objective.

The FCA has a number of powers to pursue their competition mandate, they can make rules in support of their objective to promote competition to benefit consumers or take action against firms that they regulate.

2.4.2   FCA Handbook

The FCA and PRA divided the previous Handbook to constitute their individual handbooks. If printed in their entirety, they are immense, so there are online tools which help firms to create a tailored handbook specific to their particular business, ie, areas of approved activities.

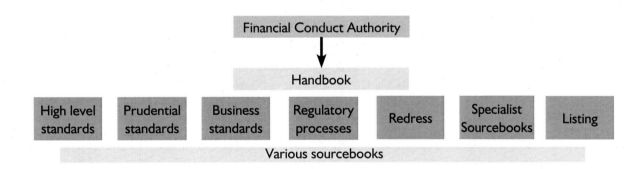

The various sourcebooks appear in the different blocks of the handbook and are referenced by their abbreviated reference code. These would be the sourcebooks which cover the activities of someone who provides investment advice and management to a private client. (It should be noted that, depending on your firm's business model and complexity, this list should not be relied upon as regulatory guidance. You must refer to your compliance department/consultants for direction.)

Handbook Block	Sourcebook	Reference code
High Level Standards	**Principles for Businesses** The fundamental obligations of all firms under regulatory system	PRIN
	Senior Management Arrangements, Systems and Controls The responsibilities of directors and senior management	SYSC
	Threshold Conditions The minimum standards for becoming and remaining authorised	COND
	Statements of Principle and Code of Practice for Approved Persons The fundamental obligations of approved persons	APER
	The Fit and Proper Test for Approved Persons The fundamental standards for becoming and remaining an approved person	FIT
	General Provisions Interpreting the Handbook, fees, approval by the FCA, emergencies, status disclosure, the FCA logo and insurance against fines	GEN
	Fees Manual The fees provisions for funding the FCA, FOS and FSCS	FEES
Prudential Standards	**Interim Prudential Sourcebook for Investment Business** The prudential requirements for investment firms	IPRU-INV
Business Standards	**Conduct of Business Sourcebook** The conduct of business requirements applying to firms with effect from 1 November 2007	COBS
	Market Conduct Code of Market Conduct, price stabilisation rules, Inter professional conduct, Endorsement of the Takeover code, Alternative Trading systems, what is acceptable market conduct and what is market abuse	MAR
	Client Assets The requirements relating to holding client assets and client money	CASS
	Training and Competence The commitments and requirements concerning staff competence	TC

Handbook Block	Sourcebook	Reference code
Regulatory processes	**Supervision** Supervisory provisions including those relating to auditors, waivers, individual guidance, notifications and reporting	SUP
	Decisions, Procedures and Penalties The FCA's procedures for taking various actions	DEPP
	Enforcement The FCA's enforcement activity against firms	EG
Redress	**Dispute Resolution: Complaints** The detailed requirements for handling complaints and the Financial Ombudsman Service arrangements	DISP

The sourcebooks provide six different provisions and these are indicated by a single letter next to the text:

R. Rules – a firm contravening these may be subject to discipline.
D. Direction – binding on those to whom they are addressed.
P. Statements of Principle for Approved Persons (APs) and binding on all APs.
C. Paragraphs which outline behaviour which does not constitute market abuse.
E. Evidential provision, a rule not binding in its own right but which relates to another binding rule.
G. Guidance to explain the implications or suggest a possible way to be compliant. A firm cannot be disciplined for failure to follow guidance.

Using this information and being able to navigate the Handbook allows you to look in more detail at the regulations, thus becoming more familiar with regulatory concepts and how this impacts on private client advice.

2.4.3 Powers of the FCA

FSMA 2000 gave the FSA, and its successor the FCA, the power to issue a number of different notices; the regulator has various tools at its disposal designed to enforce the requirements of the rules, regulations and legislation, and these are outlined for firms in SUP, DEPP and EG. Actions can be taken against authorised firms and/or individuals and so its important that APs are aware of their regulatory responsibilities and what may happen to them if they contravene the rules.

There are a variety of statutory notices which can be issued to firms and/or individuals:

*   **Warning notices** – provide details of what the FCA proposes to do and the recipients have the right to make representations as to why the FCA should not take that action.
*   **Decision notices** – give details of what the FCA will do, but include the right of appeal.
*   **Further decision notice** – agreement has taken place after discussion after the original decision notice. A further decision notice can only be issued with the recipient's consent.
*   **Notices of discontinuance** – let the recipient know that the FCA, after having previously sent warning and/or decision notices, is taking no further action.
*   **Final notices** – published on the website these set out the final actions the FCA will take.

- **Supervisory notices** – give details of what action has taken place. These are published and must be preceded by a warning or decision notice.

The first we normally see of these actions against firms is a press release which summarises the details which will be included in the attached final notice. As previously mentioned, the notice will always, where possible point towards a Principle that has been broken because the Principles for Businesses are given the status of rules (see Chapter 4 for details of the Principles for Businesses).

Regulatory Decisions Committee

Rather than the FCA Enforcement Team making decisions which are implemented in the notices listed above, the decisions are made by the Regulatory Decisions Committee (RDC).

The RDC is an independent body. Apart from the chairman, none of the members of the RDC is an FCA employee. The members comprise:

a. current and recently retired practitioners with financial services industry skills and knowledge, and
b. other suitable individuals representing the public interest.

This should facilitate an environment whereby independent decisions are made as to whether further action is required in cases where a breach of rules is suspected. The RDC is the body responsible for statutory notices, but it is not responsible for gathering the evidence itself. The FCA Enforcement Team will bring cases to the RDC, including recommendations for action, with respect to the following areas:

- Restriction of regulated activities.
- Refusal of an application for Part 4A permission.
- Refusal of approved person status.
- Making a prohibition order.
- Imposition of a financial penalty, public censure or restitution order.

Any decisions not taken by the RDC will be taken under executive procedures (where the FCA uses statutory powers). An example of this would be the imposition of a requirement on firms to submit regular reports on trading results, management accounts and customer complaints.

When determining whether or not to take disciplinary action, the regulator will consider the full circumstances relevant to the case. However, businesses concerned with the provision of advice or investment management service to private clients should remember the statutory objective of the FCA, to provide appropriate protection to clients.

Disciplinary Measures

1. **Private warnings**
   These are issued when formal disciplinary action is not deemed appropriate, but the firm/persons involved should be made aware that they were close to it. Perhaps it was a minor matter or remedial action had already been taken. The FCA requires the recipient to acknowledge receipt of the letter.
2. **Variation of permission**
   The FCA may vary the Part 4A permission previously awarded for regulated activities if:
   i. the firm is failing to satisfy threshold conditions for that activity;
   ii. the firm has not conducted the relevant activity for at least 12 months;

iii. it is necessary for the protection of consumers.
3. **Withdrawal of authorisation**
   The FCA will consider this action where it is seriously concerned about the firm or its conduct, or where the firm has finished conducting regulated activities.
4. **Withdrawal of approval**
   This prevents an approved person from continuing in the controlled function that the approval originally related to. The FCA must issue a warning notice to all interested parties on proposal, and then a decision notice on deciding. Any interested party can refer it to the Financial Services and Markets Tribunal (FSMT). Once a final notice is issued, the FCA may publish the decision.
5. **Prohibition of individuals**
   The FCA can prevent any individual, approved or not, from undertaking a function in relation to regulated activities. It would happen when it appeared that the individual is no longer fit and proper. The prohibition order could prevent a person's employment by a firm or simply restrict the functions he may undertake. Similar to withdrawal of approval, the FCA must issue a warning notice and a decision notice. When a final notice is issued, the prohibition can be published. The individual can refer to the FSMT.
6. **Public censure and statement of misconduct**
   This will be issued on firms or approved person where the FCA believes it has contravened a requirement imposed on it by FSMA 2000. A warning notice would be issued prior to the publication of the censure or statement.
7. **Financial penalties**
   This would be considered if:
   i. a firm has contravened a requirement under FSMA 2000;
   ii. an approved person is guilty of misconduct;
   iii. any person has engaged in market abuse;
   iv. a company or a director has contravened the listing rules.
   Fines are regarded as a considerable deterrent to non-compliant behaviour, especially as they are publicly disclosed. However, the amounts vary depending on the circumstances. Again warning, decision and final notices are required beforehand.

Anyone receiving a decision notice or supervisory notice has the right to refer the FCA's decision to the FSMT within 28 days, and during this time the FCA can take no action.

2.4.4   Powers of Redress on Behalf of Consumers

The power of the FCA to gain redress for customers is granted through FSMA 2000 and indeed the ability of clients to sue for damages on behalf of themselves.

- S56 FSMA gives the FCA the power to issue a prohibition order.
- S71 FSMA gives an individual the power to sue if he suffers a loss a result of a breach of the following:
  - S56(6) involves a firm or individual acting in contravention of a prohibition order;
  - S59(1) involves a firm allowing an individual to carry on a controlled function without authorisation;
  - S59(2) involves a firm allowing a contractor to carry on a controlled function without authorisation;
  - S150 allows an individual to sue if he suffers a loss as a result of the firm contravening an FCA rule.

However, it is S397 FSMA (now replaced by S89–94 FSA 2012) which is of particular relevance to the private client adviser. The section covers the Misleading Statements and Practices and this makes it an offence to make false, deceptive or misleading statements to induce another person into an investment.

CASE STUDY

A stockbroker tells a potential client that the shares of ABC (a casino company) are very cheap because ABC has just won the contract to provide a casino at Wembley. If the details of the contract were false, S89–94 of the FSA 2012 could be used to punish the stockbroker for making false and misleading statements to persuade a potential client to purchase shares.

Whilst this is a very simple example to demonstrate the point, private client advisers have to be on their guard to ensure that they do not overstate the case for an investment. It should also be noted that the law is there to protect, not just existing clients, but also potential clients.

There are however, three defences against the charge:

1. The person reasonably believed his act would not create an impression that was false or misleading.
2. After certain disclosures to investors, this may have been a method of price stabilisation in line with the FCA's rules.
3. The forecasts were made in line with 'control of information' rules laid down by the FCA. This defence may also include the use of Chinese Walls.

2.5   MONEY ADVICE SERVICE (MAS)

The Money Advice Service (MAS) is an independent organisation whose statutory objectives are to enhance the understanding and knowledge of members of the public about financial matters (including the UK financial system), and to enhance the ability of members of the public to manage their own financial affairs.

It is paid for by a statutory levy on the financial services industry, raised through the FCA.

3.   EUROPEAN AND OTHER LEGISLATION

3.1   INTRODUCTION

The UK, as a member state of the EU, plays an important part and crucial role in attempting to create a single market across European financial services. Directives issued by the European Parliament are issued to member state for implementation into their own legislation. In the case of the UK, these directives are reflected within the Handbook.

Many of the EU directives are applied to the European Economic Area (EEA), which is wider than the EU. Currently, the EU comprises 28 member states, namely:

Austria, Belgium, Bulgaria, Czech Republic, Republic of Cyprus, Denmark, Estonia, Finland, France, Greece, Hungary, Ireland, Italy, Latvia, Lithuania, Luxembourg, Malta, The Netherlands, Poland, Portugal, Romania, Republic of Slovenia, Slovak Republic, Spain, Sweden, United Kingdom and Germany.

The EEA comprises the EU plus three additional countries (Iceland, Norway and Liechtenstein).

3.2 FINANCIAL SERVICES ACTION PLAN (FSAP)

The FSAP is a key component of the European Union's attempt to create a single market for financial services. Created in 1999 and to last for a period of six years, it contained 42 articles related to the harmonisation of the financial services markets within the European Union. It was scheduled to be completed by the end of 2004.

The European Council, held in Cardiff in June 1998, requested the European Commission *'to table a framework for action....to improve the single market in financial services, in particular examining the effectiveness of implementation of current legislation and identifying weaknesses which may require amending legislation'*.

The European Commission responded with five imperatives for action that were agreed at the Vienna European Council in December 1998, and the Financial Services Action Plan was issued by the European Commission on 11 May 1999. The cornerstone of the action plan's achievement is the Markets in Financial Instruments Directive (MiFID).

 What do you think this means for private clients in the UK?

Clients should be able to purchase products and services from anywhere in the EU and be afforded the same rights irrespective of from where the products and services were purchased.

How will this change the role of the financial adviser, if the universe of products and services to chose from, increases?

What is the case for harmonisation, and what are the perceived benefits for clients? What opportunities do you believe it affords to firms who offer products and services to clients across the EU? Use the information which follows, to consider your response.

3.3 MARKETS IN FINANCIAL INSTRUMENTS DIRECTIVE (MIFID)

The Investment Services Directive issued in 1993 specified that firms had to be authorised in one member state, to provide investment services. This single authorisation allowed firms to provide those services in other member states, without the need for further authorisation. This principle is known as 'passporting'.

This directive was superseded in the UK on 1st November 2007 by the Markets in Financial Instruments Directive (MiFID). The two principal goals of the MiFID are:

1. Extend the scope of the passport to include a wider range of services.
2. Remove the major barrier to cross-border business through application of host state rules to incoming passported firms.

3.3.1   MiFID Core and Ancillary Services

Previously under the ISD, only a limited number of investment services were included in those that could be passported. Under MiFID, this list expanded and in doing so created the core activities which can be passported, namely:

*   investment advice;
*   some underwriting activities;
*   operating an MTF (multilateral trading facility – retail versions of which are coming on line currently);
*   activities relating to commodity derivatives;
*   portfolio management;
*   dealing on own account;
*   execution of orders on behalf of clients.

Additionally, there are services which cannot be passported in their own right. In these cases the service must be provided in conjunction with a core service as above:

The services which cannot be passported in their own right are:

*   safe custody;
*   granting credit to investors;
*   advising on capital structures, mergers & acquisitions;
*   foreign exchange services;
*   investment research.

3.3.2   Home State vs. Host State Regulation

MiFID makes a distinction between a firm's home state and its host state when engaging in cross-border activities. The home state is that which regulates the firm, and the host state is the EEA territory in which the firm is operating.

If the firm is operating in the host state from its base in its home state, then it is the home state regulations that must be followed. If the firm sets up a branch in the host state, the host state conduct of business rules must be observed for all investment business carried out by the branch in the host state.

In reality, this means that it is not necessary to comply with 28 different EU states, but only the conduct of business rules and these have harmonised to a greater extent, with the implementation of the MiFID legislation in 2007.

3.3.3 Financial Instruments Covered by MiFID

MiFID applies only to activities in relation to specified financial instruments. These are:

- transferable securities ie, shares, bonds and other securities giving the right to acquire shares and/or bonds;
- units in collective investment undertakings;
- money market instruments;
- financial futures contracts;
- forward interest rate agreements (FRAs);
- interest rate and currency swaps;
- options to acquire or dispose of any of the above, including currencies and interest rates;
- commodity derivatives including OTC commodity derivatives with a cash-settled option other than on default or termination. Other OTC commodity derivatives which are physically settled, which are not for commercial purposes;
- credit derivatives;
- financial CFDs.

3.4 CAPITAL REQUIREMENTS DIRECTIVE (CRD)

The CRD 'recasts' (amends and restates) the earlier Capital Adequacy Directive (CAD) and Banking Code Directive, and came into force on 1 January 2007. It is applied to banks, building societies and most investment firms.

The premise of the directive built upon ISD belief that a customer in the EU should be under no greater risk of a firm becoming insolvent, than if they had placed their business with a home state firm.

It is designed to ensure that firms hold adequate resources and have adequate systems and controls to manage both their business and its associated risks. The amount of financial resource will depend on the business carried out, the size of the business, its activities and the risks those activities give rise to. Also factored in to this calculation will be scope, products and services. This captures what is referred to as the 'three pillars'.

Quantification of risks arising for financial firms trading and credit businesses.	Series of robust requirements on public disclosure by firms, to encourage a stronger role for market discipline in ensuring that firms hold capital appropriate to their business	Stronger constructive dialogue between regulators and firms on the risks run by the latter, and the level of capital which should be held to support them.

4. FCA PRINCIPLES FOR BUSINESSES AND STATEMENTS OF PRINCIPLES

4.1 PRINCIPLES FOR BUSINESSES

The FCA has set out 11 Principles for Businesses that apply to every firm conducting a regulated activity. Some Principles apply to all authorised firms regulated by the FCA, and some only apply to firms carrying on specific business ie, advising clients and/or managing discretionary portfolios (see Principle 9).

These are a general statement of the fundamental obligations of firms under the regulatory system, and also form the foundation for the 'fit and proper' test for firms and individuals.

1.	Integrity	A firm must conduct its business with integrity.
2.	Skill, care and diligence	A firm must conduct its business with due skill, care and diligence.
3.	Management and control	A firm must take reasonable care to organise and control its affairs responsibly and effectively, with adequate risk management systems.
4.	Financial prudence	A firm must maintain adequate financial resources.
5.	Market conduct	A firm must observe proper standards of market conduct.
6.	Customers' interests	A firm must pay due regard to the interests of its customers and treat them fairly.
7.	Communications with clients	A firm must pay due regard to the information needs of its clients, and communicate information to them in a way which is clear, fair and not misleading.
8.	Conflicts of interest	A firm must manage conflicts of interest fairly, both between itself and its customers and between a customer and another client.
9.	Customers: Relationships of trust	A firm must take reasonable care to ensure the suitability of its advice and discretionary decisions for any customer who is entitled to rely upon its judgment.
10.	Clients' assets	A firm must arrange adequate protection for clients' assets when it is responsible for them.
11.	Relations with regulators	A firm must deal with its regulators in an open and co-operative way, and must disclose to the FCA appropriately, anything relating to the firm of which the FCA would reasonably expect notice.

If a firm breaches a Principle it will be liable to disciplinary sanctions, but the onus is on the FCA to show that the firm has been at fault.

 Do these Principles appear to be reasonable expectations of firms' behaviour?

Most people would look at this list and say that the Principles are nothing more than what a customer would expect. However, the FCA has found, over time, that many firms have been in breach of these Principles, in particular Principle 6 (customer interests), thus the Treating Customers Fairly initiative which began to try and encourage firms to 'do the right thing'.

We look more closely at TCF and acting in client's best interest in Chapter 6, but, commonly, those interviewed by the FCA are not able to explain how these Principles are actually met within their business. Try the following exercise.

 Look at the Principles, and try to think of a positive indicator of that Principle being met and a negative indicator demonstrating that the Principle is being breached. Consider the systems and controls you have in place in your own business, and examples of published cases where firms were found to be breaching the Principles.

Principle	Positive Indicator	Negative Indicator
Integrity – a firm must conduct itself with integrity.		
Skill, care and diligence – a firm must conduct its business with due skill, care and diligence.		
Management Control – a firm must take reasonable care to organise and control its affairs responsibly and effectively, with adequate risk management systems.		
Financial Prudence – a firm must maintain adequate financial resources.		
Market conduct – a firm must observe the proper standards of market conduct.		
Customers' interests – a firm must pay due regard to the interests of its customers, and treat them fairly.		
Communications with clients – a firm must pay due regard to the information needs of its clients, and communicate information to them in a way which is clear, fair and not misleading.		
Conflicts of interest – a firm must manage conflicts of interest both between itself and its customers and between a customer and another client.		
Customers: relationships of trust – a firm must take reasonable care to ensure the suitability of its advice and discretionary decisions for any customer who is entitled to rely upon its judgement.		
Clients' Assets – a firm must arrange adequate protection for clients' assets when it is responsible for them.		
Relations with regulators – a firm must deal with its regulators in an open and cooperative way and must disclose to the FCA appropriately, anything relating to the firm of which the FCA would reasonably expect notice.		

4.2 STATEMENTS OF PRINCIPLE AND CODE OF PRACTICE

The FCA has taken the approach that a firm is typically a collection of individuals, and, because of the importance of some of the roles carried out by some of these individuals, there are certain standards to which they must adhere. So the APER sourcebook lays out the Statements of Principle for Approved Persons. Additionally, there is a Code of Practice to help assess whether a person's conduct complies with the Statements of Principle.

4.2.1 The FCA's Approach to Approved Persons and Specifying Controlled Functions

For **dual-regulated firms**, the FCA specifies all of the significant influence functions (SIFs) that the previous regulator (FSA) did.

For **single-regulated firms** the FCA specifies all existing SIF functions (excluding the actuarial controlled functions CF12: actuarial function, CF12A: with-profits actuary and CF12B: Lloyd's actuary).

The FCA also specifies the existing customer function (CF30), which applies to both dual-regulated and single-regulated firms. The FCA will undertake a review on what longer-term changes are necessary to the approved persons' regime.

There is one particular controlled function that will fall within the FCA's area of responsibility, the mortgage customer function (CF31). The FCA remains committed to the outcomes to achieve the introduction of CF31 (ie, to help to clamp down on mortgage fraud to make all mortgage advisers personally accountable, requiring them to demonstrate they are fit and proper, and to enable the FCA and the industry to track individuals as they move between firms).

The five types of controlled function are:

1. **Governing functions** – these are the persons responsible for directing the affairs of the business. If the business is a company then they will be the directors of that company. If the business is a partnership, then they will be the partners. It is important to remember, however, that the deciding factor is not just whether the person has the title of director – someone who acts as a director, even if they are not formally registered as such (for example a **shadow director**) will also require PRA/FCA approval because of the influence they exert over the firm.
2. **Required functions** – these are specific individual functions which the PRA/FCA expects every firm to have, if it is appropriate to the nature of the business. For example, every firm should have appointed someone to fulfil the compliance oversight function and the ML reporting function. The individual tasked with performing the apportionment and oversight function (CF8) does not need to be an approved person.
3. **Systems and controls functions** – these are the functions which provide the governing body with the information it needs to meet the requirements of Principle 3 of the Principles for Businesses (see Section 1.1).
4. **Significant management function** – this function only occurs in larger firms, if there is a layer of management below the governing body, which has responsibility for a significant business unit, for example, the head of equities, the head of fixed income and the head of settlements. Until recently, several different significant management functions were identified, but now they have been merged into one.

All of the above groups are described by the FCA as **SIFs** as the persons fulfilling these roles exercise a significant influence over the conduct of a firm's affairs.

5. **Customer function** – this function involves giving advice on dealing, arranging deals and managing investments. The individuals have contact with customers in fulfilling their role. Examples of customer functions are an investment adviser, the customer trading function and the investment management function.

Customer functions are not SIFs.

The table below sets out Part 1 of the FCA-controlled functions (FCA-authorised persons and appointed representatives).

Type	CF	Description of controlled function
FCA-governing functions*	1	Director function
	2	Non-executive director function
	3	Chief executive function
	4	Partner function
	5	Director of unincorporated association function
	6	Small friendly society function
FCA-required functions*	8	Apportionment and oversight function
	10	Compliance oversight function
	10A	CASS operational oversight function
	11	Money laundering reporting function
	40	Benchmark submission function
	50	Benchmark administration function
Systems and control function*	28	Systems and controls function
Significant management function*	29	Significant management function
Customer-dealing function	30	Customer function
	31	Mortgage customer function
*FCA-significant influence functions		

The table below sets out Part 2 of the FCA-controlled functions (PRA-authorised persons).

Type	CF	Description of FCA controlled function
FCA-required functions*	8	Apportionment and oversight function
	10	Compliance oversight function
	10A	CASS operational oversight function
	11	Money laundering reporting function
	40	Benchmark submission function
	50	Benchmark administration function
Significant management function*	29	Significant management function
Customer-dealing function	30	Customer function
*FCA-significant influence functions		

The table below sets out the PRA-controlled functions for a PRA-authorised firm.

Type	CF	Description of PRA controlled function
PRA-governing functions*	1	Director
	2	Non-executive director function
	3	Chief executive function
	4	Partner
	5	Director of an unincorporated association
	6	Small friendly society
PRA-required functions*	12	Actuarial function
	12A	With-profits actuary function
	12B	Lloyd's actuary function
Significant management function*	28	Systems and controls function
*PRA-significant influence functions		

So, when a person submits their PRA SIF application, they will be required to declare if they also need approval for one of the FCA functions (see table above). This information is required so that the PRA can assess the person's suitability to perform both roles. As FCA consent is required before the PRA can approve an application, the FCA will also be involved in the assessment process. On approval by the PRA the individual's PRA-controlled function will include the FCA role. Only the PRA-controlled function will be shown on the public register.

Both the PRA and the FCA will be able to refuse the application.

To give an example, where someone is appointed to be both a chief executive and a (board level) executive director, they will only need to apply to the PRA for the chief executive function (CF3). They would not also need separate approval for CF1, as they would have under the FSA. However, the PRA's chief executive function will also cover the individual's actions as an executive director.

4.2.2 Fit and Proper

Individuals working for authorised firms who perform a controlled function (a function relating to the carrying on of a controlled activity) are required to obtain approved person status from the FCA.

The FCA will only grant approval to persons whom it deems to be fit and proper (and may withdraw approval if it deems the person no longer fit and proper). If the FCA refuses to grant approval, the matter may be referred to the Financial Services and Markets Tribunal.

In assessing fitness and propriety, the most important considerations will be the person's:

- honesty, integrity and reputation;
- competence and capability; and
- financial soundness.

Approved person status must be obtained from FCA **prior to** appointment to undertake a controlled function, and the FCA must be informed within seven days if an approved person stops performing the controlled function.

Before hiring a new employee, a firm needs to ensure that credit and CRB checks are undertaken. This will hopefully uncover those who are financially unsound or have previously been involved in fraudulent activity.

Recently, the FCA has made it clear that it will conduct telephone interviews with those applying to become SIFs. This process has led to a significant increase in the number of applications being declined.

4.2.3 Statements of Principle

Principles 1 to 4 apply to all approved persons, and Principles 5 to 7 only apply to those approved to perform significant influence functions.

Statement of Principle 1
An approved person must **act with integrity** in carrying out his controlled function.

Statement of Principle 2
An approved person must **act with due skill, care and diligence** in carrying out his controlled function.

Statement of Principle 3
An approved person must observe **proper standards of market conduct** in carrying out his controlled function.

Statement of Principle 4
An approved person must **deal with the FCA and with other regulators** in an open and co-operative way and must disclose appropriately any information of which the FCA would reasonably expect notice.

Statement of Principle 5

An approved person **performing a significant influence function** must take reasonable steps to ensure that the business of the firm for which he is responsible in his controlled function, is **organised** so that it can be **controlled effectively**.

Statement of Principle 6

An approved person **performing a significant influence function** must exercise **due skill, care and diligence in managing** the business of the firm for which he is responsible in his controlled function.

Statement of Principle 7

An approved person **performing a significant influence function** must take reasonable steps to ensure that the business of the firm for which he is responsible in his controlled function, **complies** with the relevant requirements and standards of the regulatory system.

4.2.4   Code of Practice

The Code sets out descriptions of conduct which, in the FCA's opinion, do not comply with the relevant Statements of Principle. The Code also sets out certain factors which are to be taken into account in determining whether an approved person's conduct complies with a particular Statement of Principle.

Some may agree that private client advisers, who are in a position of trust with clients and responsible for their assets, should pay particular attention to perceived breaches of these Principles. It should be noted that this is not a comprehensive list of conduct which does not comply with the Principles, and we would recommend additional reading of the APER sourcebook.

Principle 1

Deliberately misleading (or attempting to mislead) a client, the firm or the FCA and/or deliberately falsifying documents or misleading a client about performance of investments.

Principle 2

Failing to inform a customer or the firm, of material information (eg, risks or charges) in circumstances where he should provide it.

Principle 3

A factor to be taken into account in determining whether or not an approved person's conduct complies with this Statement of Principle is whether he, or his firm, has complied with relevant market codes and exchange rules.

Principle 4

Deliberately preparing inaccurate or inappropriate records or returns in connection with a controlled function, eg, performance reports, training records or details of qualifications, inaccurate trade confirmations.

Principle 5

Deliberately misusing the assets or confidential information of a client or a firm, eg, front running or churning.

Principle 6
Deliberately designing transactions so as to disguise breaches or requirements and standards.

Principle 7
Deliberately failing to disclose the existence of a conflict of interest in connection with dealings with a client.

4.3 TRAINING AND COMPETENCE

4.3.1 Introduction

In line with the MiFID article 5 which discusses the knowledge, skills and expertise of employees, the regulator has revised the Training and Competence sourcebook and it should now be read in conjunction with the Systems and Control sourcebook in which it states;

'A firm must employ personnel with the skills, knowledge and expertise necessary for the discharge of the responsibilities allocated to them.' (SYSC 3.1.6)

This covers all firms, and the revised rules relating to Training and Competence also apply to firms where its employee carries on an activity for retail clients, customers or consumers.

4.3.2 Attaining Competence, Appropriate Examinations and Supervision

A firm should not assess a person as competent to carry on any of a specified range of activities, until they have demonstrated competence and passed each module of an appropriate examination.

Firms must not allow employees to do any of the following, without having passed each module of an appropriate examination:

- certain 'advising and dealing' activities;
- acting as a broker fund adviser;
- advising on syndicate participation at Lloyds;
- acting as a pension specialist.

Until such time as the employee is deemed competent they must be appropriately supervised and that those supervising employees, have the necessary coaching and assessment skills as well as technical knowledge to act as competent supervisors and assessors.

4.3.3 Maintaining Competence

A firm must review employees' competence on a regular and frequent basis, and take appropriate action to ensure that they remain competent for their roles, and specifically take into account:

- the employees' technical knowledge and its application;
- the employees' skills and expertise;
- changes in products, legislation and regulation.

4.3.4   Record-Keeping

A firm must make appropriate records to demonstrate compliance with the rules in this sourcebook, and keep them for the following periods after an employee stops carrying on the activity:

- at least five years for MiFID business;
- three years for non-MiFID business; and
- indefinitely for a pension transfer specialist.

5.   CONDUCT OF BUSINESS RULES

5.1   INTRODUCTION

The Conduct of Business Sourcebook (Business Standards block) has wider-ranging rules and guidance on a variety of activities, many of which directly affect the way firms deal with private clients. MiFID has had a significant effect on this section of the Handbook. The new COBS sourcebook is actually shorter than the old COB sourcebook and is a good example of the desire to move to MPBR (more principle-based regulation) where there is a shift of emphasis from detailed rules to principles and high level rules and guidance.

COBS apply to firms carrying on the relevant activities (see Section 5.1.1) from an establishment maintained by them in the UK. They also apply to a firm's MiFID business carried on from an establishment in another EEA state, but only where that business is carried on within that state. So for an EEA MiFID investment, COBS rules that relate to MIFID business, do so only where that business is carried on from an establishment in the UK.

Another change to COBS from November 2008 was the inclusion of appointed representatives.

Finally before we look at the detail of the sections of COBS which directly affect advisers, wherever the rules talk about information being transmitted in a durable medium, this means paper or any instrument which allows the recipient to store it unchanged for an appropriate time, ie, on PC but not the internet unless it is held in a storage area with the ability to retrieve it.

What follows are only highlights from the COBS sourcebook with some of the issues that you will be expected to know. Reference to our learning material including the FCA's handbook itself, is recommended.

5.1.1   Activities Subject to COBS

The activities covered are:

- accepting deposits;
- designated investment business;
- long-term insurance business in relation to life policies;
- activities relating to the above.

5.2   CLIENT CLASSIFICATION (COBS 3)

Under COBS, clients are generally categorised as:

- retail, or
- professional, or
- eligible counterparties.

In reality, since these new classifications came into force, it is much harder for retail clients to opt up to professional clients. However, they can be reclassified on a transaction-by-transaction basis.

In all cases, new clients have to be informed of the classification which the firm has given to them, and the greatest level of protection must be afforded to retail clients.

If clients do wish to opt up, they must be able to meet two criteria from a quantitative test, to become Elective professional clients;

- Average trade frequency of > ten per quarter over previous four quarters.
- Portfolio worth > €500,000.
- Works, or is involved, in financial sector for > one year in a professional capacity.

Furthermore, the firm must apply a qualitative test, whereby it assesses the expertise, experience and knowledge of the client.

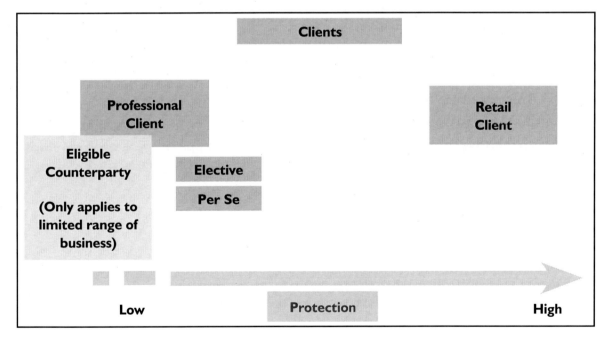

5.3   COMMUNICATING WITH CLIENTS (COBS 4)

You will see more about the concepts upon which these rules are based in Section 6 in relation to TCF and acting in the client's best interest. We need to remember Principle 6 and 7.

 Can you remember Principle 6 & 7 from Section 4? If not, go back and review them and make sure you are confident that you can relate the Principles to the rules outlined in this chapter.

5.3.1   Fair, Clear and Not Misleading

Underpinning the rules relating to advisers dealing with clients, is 'fair, clear and not misleading' which is at the core of the financial promotion rules, and the information that we send to clients. Firms must ensure that

- the firm's regulator, ie, the FCA, is named, and where matters are not regulated by the FCA, that it says so;
- financial promotions which deal with products or services where the client's capital is at risk, must say this;
- those quoting yields must give a balanced view of both short-term and long-term prospects;
- if an investment is complex, it must be clearly explained;
- where communications relate to a packaged product, that the provider of that product is accurately fairly and clearly described.

5.3.2   Communicating with Retail Clients

Generally speaking, firms have to make sure they do not disguise, diminish or obscure important items, statements or warnings.

So when firms outline past performance, they must make sure that it is not any more prominent than other information, it covers at least five years or since launch, and it shows the effects of charges and commission. With simulated performance, it needs to say that it simulated and on what it is based. With future performance, it must say on what it is based, and there must be a prominent warning that it is not a reliable indicator of future returns.

All firms should ensure that approval for financial promotions is completed by an appropriate individual.

5.3.3   Information Requirements when Managing Investments

Firms providing portfolio management services must establish a meaningful way of evaluating, and subsequently reporting on, the performance. This should be accessible by the client and would include appropriate benchmarks based on the clients' objectives and the type of investments used. When managing on behalf of retail clients, firms must:

- state the method and frequency of valuations;
- detail any delegation of the discretionary portfolio;
- state the benchmarks the portfolio is assessed against;
- state the types of designated investments and the types of transactions which may be carried out, including any limit details or restrictions on the managers' discretion;
- state the management objectives and the level of risk that may be incurred on the client's behalf.

Where firms are holding client money or investments for retail clients, they must additional provide details of who may hold them on their behalf, what would happen if the third party became insolvent, if they are likely to be held in omnibus accounts and the safeguards around that.

5.4 ADVISING AND SELLING (COBS 9)

Rules on suitability apply when firms make personal recommendations relating to designated investments and when they manage investments. They exist to ensure that firms take all reasonable steps to see that recommendations, or decision to trade, are suitable for the client.

Suitability consists of three elements, all of which must be obtained in order to establish suitability:

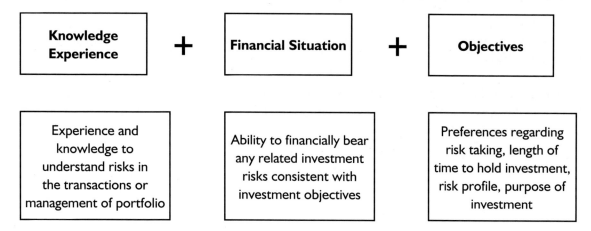

| **Knowledge Experience** | **+** | **Financial Situation** | **+** | **Objectives** |

| Experience and knowledge to understand risks in the transactions or management of portfolio | Ability to financially bear any related investment risks consistent with investment objectives | Preferences regarding risk taking, length of time to hold investment, risk profile, purpose of investment |

Suitability does not apply to execution-only business, and where the client is a professional client, firms can assume that the client has the necessary knowledge in this area.

Once suitability is established, the content of suitability reports is not prescriptive but they must explain why recommendations are suitable for the client's needs, and set out the advantages of the transaction. This report must be sent prior to the conclusion of the contract or transaction.

5.5 DEALING AND MANAGING (COBS 2, 9, 11, 12)

An important aspect of the rules for dealing and managing, is captured in the SYSC sourcebook (systems and controls) which says that firms must take all reasonable steps to identify conflicts of interest between the firm and one client of the firm or another.

5.5.1 Conflicts of Interest (SYSC 10)

Firms are therefore obliged to:

- maintain effective organisational and administrative arrangements designed to prevent conflicts;
- arrange for those producing external facing investment research, to have appropriate barriers in place to stop this information flowing to other parts of the firm;
- ensure that when conflicts cannot be managed away, that they are disclosed;
- have and maintain a conflicts policy;
- provide clients with the description of that policy;
- keep records of where conflicts have arisen.

5.5.2　Chinese Walls

SYSC requires firms to establish 'Chinese walls' if an employee holds information which must be withheld from other parts of the business. Similar to the conflicts policy, the details of this are not prescriptive so smaller firms may have far less-detailed policies than larger, more complex firms.

5.5.3　Investment Research and Recommendations

When a firm produces research, it must ensure that it is labelled or described as investment research or is otherwise presented as an objective or independent explanation of the matters contained in the recommendation.

If the recommendation in question was to be made by an investment firm to a client, it does not constitute the provision of a personal recommendation. In this instance, investment research is defined as research or other information recommending or suggesting an investment strategy, explicitly or implicitly, concerning one or several financial instruments or the issuers of financial instruments. This includes any opinion as to the present or further value or price of such instruments, intended for distribution channels or for the public.

5.5.4　Dealing Commission

Under rules about the handling of dealing commission, investment managers must not accept goods or services in addition to the execution of its customer orders, if it:

- executes its customer orders through a broker or another person;
- passes on the broker's or other person's charges to its customers;
- is offered goods or services in return for the charges referred to above.

The goods and services related to the execution of trades must be:

- linked to the arranging and conclusion of a specific investment transaction;
- provided between the point at which the investment manager makes an investment or trading decision and the point at which the investment is carried out.

Where the goods or services relate to the provision of research, the requirements of the rule on use of dealing commission are met if the research:

- is capable of adding value to the investment or trading decisions;
- represents original thought;
- has intellectual rigour;
- reaches meaningful conclusions.

There are however goods and services which the FCA does not regard as meeting the requirements, and are therefore not permissible:

- services relating to the valuation or performance measurement of portfolios;
- computer hardware;
- connectivity services such as electronic networks and dedicated telephone lines;
- seminar fees;
- subscriptions for publications;

- travel, accommodation or entertainment costs;
- order and execution management systems;
- office administrative computer software, such as word processing or accounting programmes;
- membership fees to professional associations;
- purchase or rental of standard office equipment or ancillary facilities;
- employees' salaries;
- direct money payments;
- publicly available information;
- custody services relating to designated investments belonging to, or managed for, customers, other than those services that are incidental to the execution of trades.

Any goods and services purchased through dealing commissions must be disclosed to clients before execution (prior disclosure) and periodically, at least once a year.

5.5.5 Best Execution

The landscape for best execution and a firm's policy is shifting rapidly at the moment with the rise of Multilateral Trading Facilities (MTFs), and particularly the entry into the market of retail MTFs. Firms must take all reasonable steps to obtain the best results for clients. Careful consideration must be given to:

- client category;
- client order;
- instruments involved;
- the execution venue.

Price considerations now need to include the cost of the venue, all expenses, clearing and settlements costs.

Firms are required to advise clients of their order execution policies, which will include details of all the venues that are likely to be used and the factors that will affect the choice of venue. This will need to be reviewed at least annually. You do not have to receive explicit client consent, as you only have to advise them of your policy.

5.5.6 Client Order Handling

Comparable client orders must be executed in turn, ie, the order they were received:

| Once a firm has agreed to execute a current client order, it must do so as soon as reasonably practicable | BUT the firm may postpone the order where it has taken reasonable steps to ensure that it is in the best interests of the retail client |

5.5.7 Aggregation and Allocation

Firms can only aggregate their own accounts deals with clients, or aggregate two or more clients orders if:

- It is likely that the aggregation will benefit each of the clients whose orders have been aggregated.
- The possibility has been notified to the client that it may sometimes work to their disadvantage.

The firm must have an order execution policy in place.

5.5.8 Compliance for Investment Managers and Firms Receiving and Transmitting Orders

Firms and senior managers in firms need to have systems and controls and reporting mechanism to ensure that:

- **Investment managers** act in their clients' best interest when placing orders for them.
- **Firms** receiving or transmitting orders for clients must act in their clients' best interest.

 When considering the conflicts that may arise, how might a client be disadvantaged? Could a conflict of interest benefit certain clients?

5.6 RULES ON CANCELLATION AND RIGHT TO WITHDRAW (COBS 15)

As part of the product disclosure rules outline in Section 6.3.1, there will be references to the client's right to cancel if they wish. In all cases, records will need to be retained, indefinitely for pension transfers and FSAVCs, five years for life policies or pension cases and three years for any other investments.

Contract	Cancellation period
• a life policy (including a pension annuity, a pension policy or within a wrapper) • a contract to join a personal pension scheme or a stakeholder pension scheme • a pension contract • a contract for a pension transfer • a contract to vary an existing personal pension scheme or stakeholder pension scheme by exercising, for the first time, an option to make income withdrawals	30 calendar days
• a contract for a cash deposit ISA	14 calendar days
• to buy a unit or share in a regulated collective investment scheme (including within a wrapper or pension wrapper) • to open or transfer a child trust fund (CTF) • to open or transfer an ISA or Junior ISA • for an Enterprise Investment Scheme	14 calendar days
• accepting deposits • designated investment business	14 calendar days

5.7 REPORTING TO CLIENTS (COBS 16)

5.7.1 Occasional Reporting

The rules on occasional reporting require firms, other than those managing investments, to give adequate disclosure to clients regarding any orders carried out on their behalf. Specifically a firm must:

- provide the client, in a durable medium, with the essential information concerning the execution of the order;
- for a retail client, send the client a notice, in a durable medium, confirming the execution of the order and such of the trade confirmation information as is applicable:
  - ◦ as soon as possible and no later than the first business day following that execution; or
  - ◦ if the confirmation is received by the firm from a third party, no later than the first business day following receipt of the confirmation from the third party; and
  - ◦ supply a client, on request, with information about the status of his order.

5.7.2 Periodic Reporting

Firms managing investments are required to provide periodic statements in a durable medium, unless such statements are provided by another person. This should happen at least six-monthly, but the client can request them every three months. If the portfolio is leveraged, a statement must be sent monthly.

 Why is reporting important for: a) clients; b) the firms?

Obviously for clients it means that they can compare and contrast the performance over a period. It may prompt them to contact the adviser. It provides the firm with information about the performance and allows us to monitor our activities against other management information (MI), ie, is there a connection between decline or increase in clients depending on the performance of our advisers. Is there a correlation between statement production and increased complaints, or rise in FUMs or new client recommendations? Reporting can be a crucial monitoring tool for our business activities.

6. TCF AND ACTING IN THE CLIENT'S BEST INTEREST

6.1 FCA's JOURNEY WITH TCF

Principle 6 is the Principle on which the initiative of Treating Customers Fairly is founded:

'A firm must pay due regard to its customers and treat them fairly' is the underlying Principle for the TCF initiative. It is the responsibility of the senior management of firms to deliver this.

TCF is not about standardising client services and products across industries. This is why the FCA is not providing detailed rules for businesses, because it will be different for every type of business and business model. Instead, the regulator has focused on the desirable outcomes for customers.

Outcome 1 – Consumers can be confident that they are dealing with firms where the fair treatment of customers is central to the corporate culture.

Outcome 2 – Products and services marketed and sold in the retail market are designed to meet the needs of identified consumer groups and are targeted accordingly.

Outcome 3 – Consumers are provided with clear information and are kept appropriately informed before, during and after the point-of-sale.

Outcome 4 – Where consumers receive advice, the advice is suitable and takes account of their circumstances.

Outcome 5 – Consumers are provided with products that perform as firms have led them to expect, and the associated service is of an acceptable standard and as they have been led to expect.

Outcome 6 – Consumers do not face unreasonable post-sale barriers imposed by firms to change product, switch provider, submit a claim or make a complaint.

6.2   EXAMPLES OF CONSUMER OUTCOMES BEING DELIVERED

What firms need to do is consider these outcomes and demonstrate how they deliver them from their business model, to clients. The FCA does however help firms by providing suggestion of what the outcomes may look like.

OUTCOME 1 – EXAMPLE

1. **Reporting and analysing information from staff appraisals demonstrates that behaviours match the firm's customer-centric culture, as expressed by senior management.**

2. **The firm analyses staff remuneration. The remuneration policy includes measures around the fair treatment of consumers. Analysis of this demonstrates positive staff behaviours.**

3. **The firm collates feedback from a representative sample of staff, to understand staff views on customer fairness and to capture any recommendations and improvements. Results indicate that staff are motivated, understand how to treat customers fairly and are positive about the customer benefits that the firm delivers. The firm has established a target for this feedback. The results of this feedback drive change and the firm can evidence these actions.**

OUTCOME 2 – EXAMPLE

1. The firm has identified points within the product life cycle where the cancellation of a product could result in customer detriment. It is able to demonstrate consistently high persistency levels at these times and where performance varies, reasons are understood and do not indicate consumer fairness issues.

2. The firm has articulated what it expects the customer profile will be for its products and analysis of actual customer profiles indicates that this expectation is consistently being met. Where there is variation, the firm establishes why and reasons do not impact on customer fairness. This is tracked over time and trends are monitored.

OUTCOME 3 – EXAMPLE

1. When planning a marketing campaign, the firm uses customer panels to check the information is appropriate for the target market. The firm assesses the effectiveness of these panels using post-sale customer feedback. The results demonstrate that customers understand and are able to articulate what they have bought, know the action that they need to take and are aware of the benefits and risks of taking action. This has helped the firm to establish that communications are clear, fair and not misleading.

2. The firm has documented plans in place setting out the timing, purpose and means of planned customer contact activity. It has a record showing evidence of customers consistently receiving appropriate, timely communications, allowing them to make informed decisions.

OUTCOME 4 – EXAMPLE

1. A central specialist team assesses the quality of advice. They apply a sound approach, checking the evidence that has been gathered and appropriateness of the recommendations made. These assessments indicate very low levels of poor advice and when these do occur, prompt action is taken to improve performance.

2. The firm reviews the mix of advised sales by product type and provider, and checks the degree of concentration of sales to identify any potential sales bias. These reviews show an appropriate mix of products and providers, and the firm can demonstrate no sales bias exists.

3. The firm expects a certain percentage of recommendations to be made for products that do not attract commission, in the normal course of business. The actual proportion of such recommendations is tracked at an adviser level and is in line with expectations.

OUTCOME 5 – EXAMPLE

1. The firm has set standards for the quality and speed of service, has communicated these to customers, and monitors delivery of these standards. Results demonstrate that standards are being met. Where there are any variations, the firm understands why and these do not indicate customer fairness issues.

2. Product performance is as customers have been led to expect, or if not, the firm takes appropriate action to improve it and/or customers are kept informed of reasons why. In practice, this can involve measuring performance against the terms of the product and comparing performance to alternative products, benchmarks or competitors over an appropriate period of time.

OUTCOME 6 – EXAMPLE

1. Any barriers can be justified and are in line with customer expectations (eg, exit fees are understood by the customer and are only applied in the stated circumstances). The firm measures the application of barriers to ensure they are applied fairly.

2. The reasons for and volumes of complaints received are in-line with expectations. The firm conducts root cause analysis and takes corrective actions where appropriate. Feedback about the complaint process indicates there are no barriers to making and resolving complaints.

6.3   KNOW YOUR CUSTOMER (KYC)

It is important that, in the regulated environment, advisers are as certain as they can be that they have done a good job for clients. Advisers who are unable to evidence the collection of sufficient KYC will find it difficult to show that they have acted in the client's best interest, even if they have.

As there is no set structure for obtaining this information, it is the skill of the adviser in ascertaining the client's particular circumstances which is most important. The client must feel trust in the same way as the skilled adviser demonstrates empathy. During the course of initial discussion to establish suitability of a portfolio or product, an adviser must gather the following:

*   **Personal information** – name, address, date of birth, marital status, dependents and health.
*   **Employment** – occupation, employer's details and benefits or details of self-employment.
*   **Income** from all sources.
*   **Expenditure** – all outgoings including debt or credit card repayments.
*   **Assets** – property, valuables, savings, investments.
*   **Liabilities** – mortgage, loans, credit cards etc.
*   **Objectives** – what the client is hoping to achieve.
*   **Attitude to risk** – how much risk they are prepared to tolerate.

6.3.1   Product Disclosure (COBS 13 & 14)

When firms and advisers provide advice or personalised information about packaged products to a customer, they must provide written details of the key features of the product they are recommending.

The production of this document must be to the same standard as any marketing material with two elements:

- Key features of the product (Key Investor Information Document – KIID);
- Product illustration (key facts illustration – (KFI).

The KIID describes the product in the order of the following headings:

- **'Its aims'** – a brief description of the product's aims.
- **'Your commitment' or 'Your investment'** – what a retail client is committing to or investing in, and any consequences of failing to maintain the commitment or investment.
- **'Risks'** – the material risks associated with the product, including a description of the factors that may have an adverse effect on performance or are material to the decision to invest.
- **'Questions and Answers'** – the principal terms of the product, what it will do for a retail client and any other information necessary to enable a retail client to make an informed decision.

The KFI must cover:

- The premium or investment.
- Any guaranteed benefits, ie, sum assured.
- A projection of the final benefit, based on the FCA-specified assumed growth rate.
- Effect of charges.
- Commission payable to the adviser.

Clients have often overlooked the extent or importance of a particular need, and it is then the responsibility of the adviser to point this out, as the professional in this situation. We cannot prevent those clients who choose to ignore this, but advisers need to show that they recognised issues, highlighted them to the client and client has decided not to take up the recommendations. This all forms part of the details of the ongoing relationship, and is evidence of 'acting in the clients' best interest' at all times.

6.3.2   Retail Distribution Review (RDR)

In 2009 the then regulator (the FSA) published a consultation paper and proposals for implementing the Retail Distribution Review (RDR). The regulator was seeking to:

- improve the clarity with which firms describe their services to consumers;
- address the potential for adviser remuneration to distort consumer outcomes; and
- increase the professional standards of advisers.

Restricted advice is where an adviser can only recommend certain products, product providers or both. Therefore, they might only offer products from one company, or just one type of product. They could also focus on one particular market.

The rules on adviser charging became effective from 1 January 2013.

The approach for implementing the RDR means that it applies to advised sales for a defined range of retail products, but does not apply to non-advised business – such as execution-only and discretionary. However, firms that carry out discretionary management and provide advice as part of that service will be caught by the RDR requirements.

The requirements widened the scope of investment products that can be advised within the scope of the regime for retail investment products; the range of instruments available for advice is wider than the current packaged product regime. Notably, advisers can now provide a personal recommendation on investment trust shares, not just a regular savings scheme, as well as unauthorised collective investment trust schemes.

Advisers who are not **independent**, ie, do not select instruments from the whole of the market, will be classified as **restricted**. They must describe this restricted service to consumers, with a short description to help consumers understand the service that is being provided to them.

A firm must disclose in writing to a retail client, in good time before the provision of its services in respect of a personal recommendation or basic advice in relation to a retail investment product, whether the advice will be independent or restricted advice.

A firm that provides independent advice in respect of a relevant market that does not include all retail investment products must include in its disclosure to the retail client an explanation of that market – including the types of retail investment products which constitute that market. Where a firm provides restricted advice, its disclosure must explain the nature of the restriction. Where a firm provides both independent advice and restricted advice, the disclosure must clearly explain the different nature of the independent advice and restricted advice services.

Disclosure must be made in a durable medium or through a website. A firm is able to provide the disclosure by using a services and costs disclosure document or a combined initial disclosure document.

Where a firm provides restricted advice and engages in spoken interaction with a retail client, the firm must disclose orally, in good time before the provision of its services in respect of a personal recommendation, that it provides restricted advice and the nature of that restriction.

Advisers will not be able to be remunerated from the product provider when making a personal recommendation to a consumer. They must charge the consumer for the advice and service that they are providing. It is for the adviser and the consumer to agree the charge, prior to the service being provided by the adviser.

The adviser is prohibited from receiving **trail commission** on any new business carried out with consumers, including existing clients, as of 1 January 2013. But the adviser will be able to receive trail commission on advice provided before 31 December 2012 on legacy business.

A client can pay the adviser separately for the services, or the charge for the service can be deducted from the amount that is being invested.

The Adviser Charging rules in COBS 6.2A (Describing advice services) state that a firm must not hold itself out to a retail client as acting independently unless the only personal recommendations in relation to retail investment products it offers to that retail client are based on a comprehensive and fair analysis of the relevant market and are unbiased and unrestricted.

6.3.3   Management Information (MI)

Controls and formal procedures should be used to avoid keeping everything 'in their head'. Management information (MI) is very important in analysing trends, helping to forecast the future and solving and identifying problems.

MI could cover customers, calls, visits, meetings and much more. MI is not just about numbers – the views of a locum, customer feedback or complaints can also form an important part of MI.

MI can come in many different forms – some common types are:

- new business register;
- business persistency;
- training and competence records;
- file reviews;
- customer feedback
- compliance reports.

It may be appropriate to consider a risk-based approach, where areas of service are monitored more closely when they involve riskier products or solutions.

Standard information may be analysed differently. For example, to gauge what it shows about the fair treatment of customers, rather than the firm's financial performance.

Negative feedback or MI can often tell more about the firm and its culture than compliments will.

 What kind of Management Information do you think a group could collect to support the premise that it was treating customers fairly?

Obviously this will depend on the nature of the business and what is proportional to that business.

Can you think about examples that you would use to demonstrate that the customers' outcomes were manifestly being delivered from within an organisation?

7.   COMPLAINTS–HANDLING

7.1   RIGHT TO COMPLAIN UNDER FSMA

Even where legal action is available, it may be impractical or burdensome for smaller investors to pursue a claim against a firm through the courts. In consequence, FSMA 2000 obliges the FCA to impose requirements on firms to ensure the fair handling of complaints. It also obliges the FCA to set up a body to consider claims against a firm by its customers. This body is the Financial Ombudsman Service (FOS).

7.2   INTERNAL COMPLAINTS HANDLING PROCEDURES

A firm must have in place and operate appropriate and effective internal complaint handling procedures (which must be written down) for handling any expression of dissatisfaction whether oral or written, and whether justified or not, from or on behalf of an eligible complainant about the firm's services. This must be readily available for customers or potential customers to see at every branch or office of the firm.

In general, the internal complaints-handling procedures should provide for:

*   receiving complaints;
*   responding to complaints;
*   the appropriate investigation of complaints; and
*   notifying eligible complainants of their right to go to the FOS, where relevant.

In particular, a firm's procedures must make provision for:

*   appropriate staff to investigate the complaint;
*   the employee to have the authority to settle complaints (or have ready access to someone who can); and
*   the response by the firm to address the complaint adequately and to offer appropriate redress.

 How are customers or potential customers informed of your internal complaints procedure? How does your firm organise its complaints-handling?

We must remember that one of the customer outcomes of TCF is the ability of customers and clients to be able to make a complaint. Eligible complaints can be oral or written. Is every member of staff aware or the procedure to ensure that complaints are handled correctly and in a timely manner?

7.3   ELIGIBLE COMPLAINANTS

An eligible complainant is a person who is, or has been, a customer, or is a potential customer of the firm, and is:

*   a private individual; or
*   a business which has a group annual turnover of less than £1 million at the time of the complaint; or
*   a charity which has an annual income of less than £1 million at the time of the complaint; or
*   a trustee of a trust which has a net asset value of less than £1 million at the time of the complaint.

A claim of financial loss may relate either to actual loss or to possible future loss (eg, as a result of a mis-sold pension or endowment policy). However, complaints solely about investment performance will not be eligible for review by FOS, as they are deemed to be ineligible for compensation (caveat emptor) unless it is accompanied by the suggestion that the performance is due to incompetence or poor systems and controls, and this can be shown.

7.4   RECORD-KEEPING AND REPORTING

Records regarding complaints must be kept for a minimum of three years (five years for MiFID business), and must include the name of the complainant, the substance of the complaint and details of the correspondence.

The FCA will require twice-yearly reports on the number of complaints, broken down into categories, number of those closed, and those outstanding at the end of the period. They have recently announced that these reports are to be made public, so customers and potential customers can see the complaints against the firm.

7.5   ROLE OF THE FINANCIAL OMBUDSMAN SERVICE (FOS)

The FOS operates independently of the FCA, with a board of directors appointed by the FCA (subject, in the case of the chairman, to Treasury approval). The FOS and its staff are not crown agents, but are immune from civil actions. They must prepare an annual report for the FCA, on the discharge of its functions.

7.5.1   Procedure and Jurisdiction

The FOS will only accept cases where the complainant has first approached the firm concerned. The FOS has two jurisdictions:

Compulsory Jurisdiction
The FOS will only consider a complaint under compulsory jurisdiction regarding regulated and ancillary activities of authorised firms. Through the FOS, and in accordance with FSMA 2000, resolution must be sought via investigation and must be determined by what is 'fair and reasonable'.

Voluntary Jurisdiction
In essence, this will operate in a similar manner to the compulsory jurisdiction. The main elements are:

*   the firm must be a **willing participant**;
*   the complainant must be eligible;
*   the complaint is with regard to business not covered by compulsory jurisdiction and in respect of lending money secured on land, or financial services activities covered by a different scheme previously in existence;
*   although voluntary, the parties must still submit to any investigation deemed necessary by the FOS.

7.5.2   Redress

The FOS will decide the amount and type of any award. There may be:

*   a money award as compensation; and
*   a direction to take appropriate action.

The maximum money award is £150,000. The amount of the award may include a contribution towards the complainant's costs. If the FOS considers that an award larger than the maximum would be fair, it can recommend (but not require) the firm to pay the balance.

The decision of the FOS is binding on firms if it is accepted by the complainant.

However, if the complainant is dissatisfied with the outcome, they may seek a remedy in a court. As already outlined, firms must have explained to customers that they have the right to approach the FOS, and enclose details of how to do this, normally using the booklet that the FOS produces on how to use their services.

7.6 FINANCIAL SERVICES COMPENSATION SCHEME (FSCS)

The regulator has also set up a body called the Financial Services Compensation Scheme Ltd (FSCS) which deals with compensation claims from eligible claimants in the event of default by:

- a UK-authorised firm;
- an appointed representative; or
- an incoming passported EEA firm.

Those who have protected claims are also able to seek compensation from the FSCS. Protected claims are claims made in respect of deposits, insurance and investment business. Protected investment business means designated investment business, the activities of the manager/trustee of an Authorised Unit Trust and the activities of an Authorised Corporate Director/Depository of an ICVC.

Those that are **not** specifically mentioned as eligible complainants for compensation via the FSCS are:

- authorised firms (other than a sole trader firm, a credit union or a small business whose claim arises out of a regulated activity for which they do not have a permission);
- overseas financial services institutions;
- supranational institutions, governments, and central administrative authorities;
- provincial, regional, local and municipal authorities;
- large companies or large mutual associations.

7.6.1 Structure and Compensation Payable

FSCS is funded by the financial services industry through an annual levy paid by every firm registered with the FCA.

The level of compensation is limited and FSCS will only pay out for actual financial loss. It also depends on the product and when the claim was made. The current limits are outlined below:

- **Deposits** – first £85,000 per person per firm.
- **Investments** – first £50,000 per person per firm (for claims against firms declared in default after 1 January 2010).
- **Home finance** – first £50,000 per person per firm (for claims against firms declared in default after 1 January 2010).
- **Insurance business** – unlimited; 90% of the claim with no upper limit. Compulsory insurance is 100% protected.

Candidates can find more detailed information and updates on the FSCS website: www.fscs.org.uk.

8. FIRMS' RESPONSIBILTY FOR COMBATING FINANCIAL CRIME

Financial crime threatens both the FCA's consumer protection and market integrity objectives. The FCA is ready to take action in relation to financial crime risk in the sectors or markets it regulates. The policies and procedures that firms must have in place to help combat financial crime have an impact on clients. It is important to remember that these policies are there to deter those trying to commit financial crime, or at least make it harder for them to attempt to target firms for the purposes of crime.

8.1 INSIDER DEALING

Insider dealing can be defined as the deliberate exploitation of information by dealing in securities, having obtained that information by virtue of some privileged relationship or position. This is unfair on other market participants who will, in turn, lose confidence in the operation of the relevant market. The legislation on insider dealing is contained in Part V of the Criminal Justice Act 1993 (CJA 1993).

8.1.1 Who is an Insider?

A person who is in possession of price-sensitive information because:

1. he is an inside source; or
2. he has access to the information by virtue of his employment, position or profession; or
3. he has received information, directly or indirectly from a person who is either of 1) or 2).

8.1.2 Offences under the CJA

1. **Dealing** in price-affected **securities** on the basis of **inside information**.
2. **Encouraging** another person to do so. This is an offence even if the other person does not deal.
3. **Disclosing** the inside information, unless no dealing is expected.

These offences can only be committed by an individual, but, of course, encouraging a company to deal could be deemed to be an offence.

8.1.3   Securities Listed in the CJA

- shares;
- debt securities (including gilts);
- warrants;
- depositary receipts;
- options on securities;
- futures on securities;
- contracts for differences on securities or an index based on a basket of securities.

A professional intermediary is a person carrying on a business dealing in securities, and may not be knowingly party to any criminal activity.

8.1.4   Defences

There are three general defences against the charge of insider dealing;

1. Did not expect to make a profit;
2. Believed that information sufficiently widely held;
3. Would have dealt without the information.

In addition, there are three special defences against a charge of insider dealing to ensure that legitimate market activities are not curtailed:

1. Acted in the course of normal market making.
2. Market information.
3. Acting in accordance with 'price stabilisation' rules.

The FCA is empowered under FSMA 2000 to prosecute under the CJA. The maximum penalties are:

- **crown court** (conviction on indictment) – seven years jail and/or an unlimited fine;
- **magistrates court** (summary conviction) – six months jail and/or a £5,000 fine;

As an alternative to a prosecution for insider dealing, the FCA may take civil action under the market abuse regime.

 What are the ways that a firm can protect itself from insider dealing, either on its own shares or by its employees?

8.2   MARKET ABUSE

Market abuse may not necessarily see the movement of any securities. There are three criterion needed for there to be an offence under FSMA 2000 s.118:

1. Based on information not generally known.
2. Likely to give a false or misleading impression.
3. Likely to distort the market in that investment.

8.2.1 Offences

There are 7 offences under the Market Conduct sourcebook (MAR)

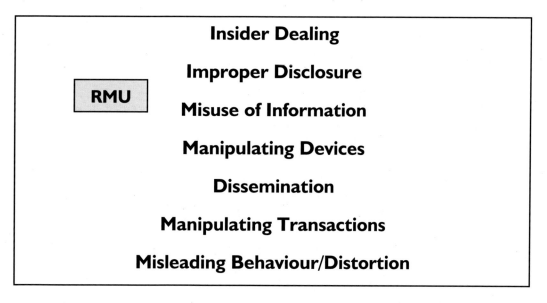

Insider Dealing

Improper Disclosure

RMU

Misuse of Information

Manipulating Devices

Dissemination

Manipulating Transactions

Misleading Behaviour/Distortion

RMU – Regular market user. Would a hypothetical reasonable person, familiar with the market in question, regard the behaviour as acceptable in the light of all the relevant circumstances?

8.2.2 Examples

To help you understand the offences, here is an example of the each offence:

1. **Insider Dealing**
   Already covered in Section 8.1.
2. **Improper Disclosure**
   X, an analyst employed by an investment bank, telephones the finance director at B plc and presses for details of the profit and loss account from the latest unpublished management accounts of B PLC.
   X is guilty of the offence of encouraging market abuse.
3. **Misuse of Information**
   X, an employee of D plc, is aware of contractual negotiations between D and a customer. Transactions with that customer have generated over 10% of D's turnover in each of the last five financial years. X knows that the customer has threatened to take its business elsewhere, and that the negotiations, whilst ongoing, are not proceeding well.
   X sells his shares in D plc.
   X is guilty of the offence of misuse of information.
4. **Manipulating Transactions**
   Effecting transactions which:
   1. give, or are likely to give, a false or misleading impression as to the supply of, or demand for, investments or as to the price of one or more qualifying investments; or
   2. secure the price or one or more such investments at an abnormal or artificial level.

A fund manager's performance is measured on the basis of the value of the portfolio at a particular time. The fund manager buys a large quantity of one of the holdings just before that time, to drive the price up.

The fund manager is guilty of market abuse.

5. **Manipulating Devices**

   Effecting transactions or orders to trade, which employ fictitious devices or any other form of deception.

6. **Dissemination**

   Dissemination of information, by any means, which gives a false or misleading impression as to a qualifying investment, by a person who knew, or could reasonably be expected to have known, that the information was false or misleading.

   Includes:

   ○ false trade reporting if reckless;
   ○ misleading information on bulletin boards;
   ○ journalists can be caught.

7. **Misleading Behaviour**

   Behaviour likely to give a regular user of the market a false or misleading impression as to the supply of, demand for or price or value of, a qualifying investment, including:

   ○ moving commodities;
   ○ moving empty cargo ships.

8.3   MONEY LAUNDERING

Defined as the process by which criminals attempt to hide and disguise the true origin and ownership of the proceeds of their criminal activities, thereby avoiding prosecution, conviction and confiscation of the criminal funds.

There is a significant amount of legislation which firms need to be aware of, but most will leave the interpretation to the MLRO (Money Laundering Reporting Officer). However, it should be noted that senior managers of firms take ultimate responsibility for their firms complying with legislation and ensuring they are doing everything they can to avoid being used to launder money.

- Proceeds of Crime Act 2002 (POCA);
- Serious organised Crime and Police Act 2005;
- Money Laundering Regulations 2007;
- Money Laundering Directive;
- Joint Money Laundering Steering Group (JMLSG) – guidance notes;
- Fraud Act 2006;
- FCA Handbook – SYSC.

8.3.1   Stages of Money Laundering

- **Placement** – introducing the criminal funds to the financial system.
- **Layering** – moving money in a series of complex transactions to mask its origins.
- **Integration** – removing the money for the benefit of the ultimate beneficiary, who appears to hold clean funds.

8.3.2 Offences

Under the POCA 2002, there are five offences, each of which carries its own penalty.

*   concealing;
*   arranging;
*   acquisition, use and possession;
*   failure to disclose;
*   tipping off.

8.3.3 Joint Money Laundering Steering Group (JMLSG) Guidance

It is the JMLSG guidance that most firms will build their internal procedures upon. However, they must be using a risk-based approach which is proportionate to their client base and their business model. This is designed to ensure that it places hurdles for those who are trying the break the law, but it is not overly burdensome for honest clients or out of step with other firms of a similar size.

The guiding principles are:

*   Obtain proof of client identities and verify these.
*   Staff training and understanding of the issues.
*   Recognition that individual staff are responsible for reporting suspicious activity.
*   Summarise the groups approach to assessing and managing money laundering and terrorist financing risks.
*   Summary of the firm's procedures to appropriate identification and monitoring checks.
*   Summarise the appropriate monitoring of policies and procedures.

 The JMLSG guidance places a lot of emphasis on the firm's KYC. Why do you think this is?

In the event of an investigation, firms will be required to provide details of their clients and money received from them. These records, coupled with the further in-depth information you should collect as part of KYC, may well hold vital information. Remember money laundering involves the funds from any criminal activity and that includes tax evasion. Senior managers have to be satisfied that they have robust internal procedures and that all advisers are adhering to them.

INVESTMENT TAXATION

An exam specification breakdown is provided at the back of this workbook

CISI
CHARTERED INSTITUTE FOR
SECURITIES & INVESTMENT

1.   INTRODUCTION

In this module we will be building on your existing understanding of the UK tax system, specifically looking at income tax, capital gains tax and inheritance tax.

Much of this will be familiar to you already, not just from your work but from your own personal tax situation. This will provide a good base to build on to look at some of the areas from a more theoretical basis that will help in your examination.

This section is also closely linked with Module 5, which looks at Financial Instruments and Products. One of the key features of these instruments and products is their tax treatment.

You must continue reading and extending your understanding around the topics covered, through additional study. This workbook does not represent everything you may be expected to know for the examination.

You will see icons or symbols alongside the text. These indicate activities or questions that have been designed to check your understanding and help you validate your understanding.

Here is a guide as to what each of the symbols means:

 Question

This identifies a question that will enable you to check your knowledge and understanding.

 Analyse

This gives you an opportunity to consider a question posed and compare your answers to the feedback given.

 Test

At the end of the module, you will have the opportunity to validate your learning by attempting questions which require knowledge of these topics.

1.1   OBJECTIVES

Income Tax

1. Understand the role of HMRC and the structure of the UK self-assessment tax system.
2. Understand when and how income tax is applied to earnings, interest and dividends and, in some cases, capital gains.
3. Be able to calculate simple tax computations.
4. Apply the main rules relating to allowable deductions, personal allowances and reliefs, marriage and civil partnerships and their breakdown, and the tax liabilities of minors.
5. Understand the tax treatment of different kinds of investments and the taxation of income arising on overseas investments.
6. Evaluate the tax efficiency of an investment asset within the wider context of suitability for an individual customer.

Capital Gains Tax

7. Understand the principles of Capital Gains Tax, and when and how it arises.
8. Understand the main CGT exemptions and reliefs available including main residence, exempt assets and exemption limits applicable for individuals, trusts and estates.
9. Understand the main disposal rules for CGT, including special rules that apply to disposals on death and between spouses/ civil partners.
10. Know the calculations applicable to assets purchased prior to, and post, 31 March 1982.
11. Be able to calculate taxable gains on an individual's net gains for a fiscal year.
12. Understand due dates for paying CGT, and the use of CGT deferral.

Inheritance Tax

13. Understand the liability to IHT, and the effects on IHT liability of chargeable lifetime transfers and transfers on death.
14. Understand IHT exemptions and reliefs, excluded assets, Potentially Exempt Transfers, and gifts with reservation.
15. Understand the rules governing the administration of estates, grant of probate and registration of probate.
16. Be able to value assets for probate and lifetime transfers.
17. Be able to calculate IHT liability based on a straightforward example.
18. Understand the relationship between the valuation of assets for CGT purposes, and valuation of assets for IHT-related chargeable lifetime and estate transfers.

Offshore Tax

19. Understand the tax treatment of onshore and offshore funds.
20. Evaluate the suitability of an offshore investment for a UK-domiciled individual.

2.   RESIDENCE AND DOMICILE

2.1   INTRODUCTION

In this section, we will concentrate on three main taxes that impact on investment decisions: Income Tax, Capital Gains Tax (CGT) and Inheritance Tax (IHT). However, it is also important to consider the individual and their status, as that can affect the rules applied for each type of tax.

Broadly, there are three status concepts that we need to be aware of:

*   resident;
*   ordinarily resident;
*   domiciled.

 Before we go on to define them, consider what you think the rules are for each, and which tax do they impact the most?

2.2   RESIDENCE

The residence status of an individual is determined separately each tax year. There are a number of specific tests to determine this, the main ones being listed below:

*   An individual will be deemed resident in the UK if they spend 183 days or more in the UK in a tax year:
    *   any day that a person is present in the UK at midnight (except if they are in transit between two places outside the UK) is counted as a day of presence.
*   If a person comes to live in the UK for three years or more they are resident from the date of arrival, and so an individual might be regarded as UK resident for the first tax year, even if they have spent less than 183 days in the UK. This would be the case if the individual comes to the UK with the intention of an indefinite stay.
*   Individuals are also treated as UK resident if they make 'habitual and substantial' visits to the UK.
    *   **Habitual** constitutes continuing for four consecutive tax years.
    *   **Substantial** is an average of 91 days or more taken over a maximum of four tax years.

As you can see from the above, it is therefore possible for an individual to be 'resident' in two countries in one tax year. It is in these situations that double-taxation agreements between countries may be brought into use to ensure an individual is not unfairly taxed on the same income or gains.

The tax that is impacted most by an individual's residence status is income tax, as anyone deemed UK resident is liable for UK income tax on worldwide earnings. Residence status can also impact on CGT liabilities.

2.3   ORDINARY RESIDENCE

The status of 'ordinary residence' is not as clearly defined as that of residence.

You would be considered to be 'ordinarily resident' if:

1. you have come to the UK voluntarily;
2. your presence has a settled purpose;
3. your presence in the UK is part of your habitual life for the time being.

Living and working in the UK for three years or more is deemed to be enough to give 'ordinary residence' status.

Effectively, the test for ordinary residence is whether an individual visits the UK as part of a regular pattern of life.

For example, former non-residents who are treated as resident under the habitual and substantial test will be treated as being ordinarily resident in the UK from the fifth tax year. This is unless it was clear from the outset that the individual intended to make habitual and substantial visits to the UK, in which case they would be treated as being ordinarily resident from outset.

Ordinary resident status similarly impacts on income tax and CGT liabilities. For example, it is important to note that individuals cannot just leave the UK for one tax year (thereby losing residence status) and avoid a UK CGT charge on disposing of assets. In this situation, they will still be liable to UK CGT on any gains realised after departure, if they:

*   have been UK resident for any part of at least four out of the last seven tax years, **AND**
*   they become non-resident or not ordinarily resident for a period of less than five tax years.

2.4   DOMICILE

The status of 'domicile' is a more permanent one than that of residence. Broadly speaking, an individual is domiciled in a country where they have their permanent home. However, an individual can often retain their domicile for the whole of their life, even if they live abroad. Although it is possible to have dual nationality or dual residence, it is not possible to have dual domicile.

An individual will initially take on a 'domicile of origin', which is acquired at birth and normally (in England and Wales) is that of the father's domicile. Illegitimate children, or those who are born after the death of their father, take on their mother's domicile. The domicile follows that of the relevant parent until age 16.

It is possible to try to establish a 'domicile of choice', by moving to a new country with the intention of living there permanently. There are no strict rules for acquiring this change of domicile; instead a number of separate factors are taken into account, such as voting in the new country, establishing a business there, making a locally valid will there, acquiring citizenship or nationality there etc.

One clear and strict rule about domicile in the UK is that of being 'deemed domicile'. HMRC will deem an individual UK-domiciled if they have been resident in the UK for 17 out of the previous 20 tax years.

The tax most affected by domicility status is IHT. Any individual who is UK-domiciled, or deemed UK-domiciled, is liable for IHT on their worldwide property. If someone is non-UK domiciled, they are only liable to IHT on their UK property. You can see from this why it is important for HMRC to be able to 'deem' someone domiciled in the UK!

2.5   LIABILITIES OF UK RESIDENTS

Broadly speaking, if an individual is classed as UK resident, ordinarily resident and domiciled, HMRC will tax that individual on all of their income, both earnings and investment income, no matter where in the world it originated. This is known as the **arising basis**.

If an individual is resident in the UK, but is not ordinarily resident and/or not UK domiciled, that individual is entitled to claim the **remittance basis** of taxation. This means that they are still taxed like other UK residents on their income and gains arising in the UK. They are also taxed on any income or gains they 'remit' to the UK (ie, bring in to the UK from overseas). However, they are not taxed on their foreign income and gains, which remain outside the UK.

From April 2008, most individuals who claim the remittance basis lost their entitlement to UK personal tax allowances, for both income tax (see Section 3.5.3) and capital gains tax (see Section 4.2.5). They also have to pay a Remittance Basis Charge of between £30,000 and £50,000 depending on how long they have been UK-resident per annum.

You will note that we said 'most' individuals are impacted by this charge. Those who are not impacted are those who:

- are under 18 years of age.
- have been resident in the UK for less than seven out of the previous nine tax years.
- have less than £2,000 unremitted foreign income and/or gains. These individuals will still have to pay UK tax on any foreign income and/or gains they remit to the UK.

3.   INCOME TAX

3.1   TYPES OF TAX

In the UK, there are different types of taxes:

- Direct taxes, which are imposed directly on the taxpayer.
  Examples of direct taxes are:
  - Income tax;
  - Capital gains tax;
  - Inheritance tax;
  - Corporation tax;
  - National Insurance.
- Indirect taxes, which are paid indirectly as part of the price of goods or services.
  Examples of indirect taxes (and there are many of them) are:
  - Value added tax (VAT);

   ○ Stamp duty land tax;
   ○ Stamp duty reserve tax;
   ○ Excise duties.

In this chapter, we will concentrate on some of the main direct taxes, and how these are collected by Her Majesty's Revenue & Customs (HMRC), whose role it is to ensure the correct tax is paid at the correct time.

 What do you think are the three main ways that direct taxes are collected from individuals?

Taxes are collected by HMRC:

- through self-assessment,
- by deduction at source through Pay As You Earn (PAYE),
- by deduction at source on savings and investment income.

3.2   SELF-ASSESSMENT

The self-assessment system of collecting tax was introduced in the UK for the tax year 1996–97. It is generally for those with more complex tax affairs – the self-employed, company directors and those liable to higher-rate tax on investment income. It is not an additional tax, just a simplified method for those people who used to have to complete several tax forms previously, and who may have been paying tax on different types of incomes at different times (even in different years!). The process allows the taxpayer the option of calculating their own tax payments, if they wish. It is estimated that just under ten million people are affected.

The direct taxes that individuals pay under self-assessment are income tax (on all types of income), Class 4 National Insurance contributions and capital gains tax.

3.2.1   Filing Dates

We have already mentioned that the self-assessment process allows a taxpayer the option of calculating their own tax payments, but they can opt for the HMRC to do the calculation for them. Either way, there are strict calendar deadlines to be met, which are tighter if the taxpayer desires the HMRC to complete the tax calculation. There are also different deadlines for filing tax returns online, or by paper.

Currently, the key dates are:

- **31 October** (following the tax year to which the return relates)
   ○ This is the deadline for filing on paper, and getting the HMRC to calculate the tax due in time for payment the following 31 January. For example, the deadline for filing a paper return in relation to tax year 2012–13 is 31 October 2013.
- **31 January** (following the tax year to which the return relates)
   ○ This is the deadline for filing online. By following the online process, the amount of tax owing will automatically be calculated. For example, the deadline for filing an online return in relation to tax year 2012–13 is 31 January 2014.

Normally tax returns are sent out by HMRC on 6 April, the first day of the new fiscal year. However, it is possible they could be sent later, particularly if they are informed about a change of circumstances for an individual. If this is the case, and the return is not received before 31 July following the tax year to which it relates, the individual has three months from the date of issue to file their return on paper. If they choose to file online, the deadline for filing is three months from the date of issue or 31 January, whichever is the later.

3.2.2   Payments on Account

Once the tax liability has been calculated, it clearly has to be paid. Rather than receive ad-hoc payments, HMRC operates a system where the tax due is paid over three dates. The first two payments are known as 'payments on account', with the third being the 'balancing payment'.

The dates of these are:

- **31 January**   First payment on account
- **31 July**   Second payment on account
- **31 January**   Balancing payment

This can sometimes appear a bit complex, as the HMRC adopt a 'current year' system which means, for example, the first payment is due in the tax year that the trading year for a self-employed individual ends. This may mean that the first payment is due before the end of the trading year.

For example, John Lewis runs his own plumbing firm, JL Pipes, which has a trading year that ends on 31 March. For tax year 2012–13, his first payment on account is due on 31 January 2014, two months before the end of his trading year!

As a result of this, an estimated value has to be used. This estimated value for the first payment on account is always half of the **previous** tax year's final due amount. The second payment on account is therefore the second half of this amount. The balancing payment will then result in more tax being paid to HMRC (if the tax due has increased) or could lead to a credit if the individual's tax bill has reduced.

Returning to the situation for JL Pipes, in 2012–13 John paid a total income tax bill of £22,000. His first payment on account, paid on 31 January 2013, is therefore £11,000. The second payment on account, paid on 31 July 2013, is also £11,000. Later in the year, John's accountant tells him that the total tax bill for 2013–14 is £26,000. As he has only paid £22,000, he needs to pay a balancing payment of £4,000 on 31 January 2014 in respect of tax due from 2013–14. On this date, of course, he must also pay the first payment on account for tax year 2014–15, which will be half of the total amount due for 2013–14. Half of £26,000 means that £13,000 will be due alongside the balancing payment.

   Try this one yourself, before checking your answers below.

Kelly is a self-employed consultant. Her income tax liability for tax year 2012–13 was £8,400, of which she has paid £6,200 on account. What amount(s) is she due to pay on 31 January 2014?

She still has £2,200 to pay as a balancing payment for tax year 2012–13. In addition, she will pay her first payment on account for tax year 2013–14, which will be £4,200 (half of the overall 2012–13 liability). So that's £6,400 in total.

3.2.3   Interest, Surcharges and Penalties

When the deadlines described above are not met, HMRC can levy interest. This is charged from the date the tax was due, usually 31 January or 31 July. The current rate of interest charged (since September 2009) is 3.0%. To be fair to HMRC, they also usually pay interest on overpaid tax. We say 'usually' because, due to the exceptionally low bank base rate, from 24 March 2009 the HMRC is not currently paying interest on overpaid tax. This position is subject to change.

A 5% surcharge is levied on tax remaining unpaid 28 days after a balancing payment is due, with a further 5% surcharge levied if the tax remains unpaid six months after the due date. These surcharges are in addition to the interest being accrued.

There are also automatic fixed penalties, for example of £100 for any return not submitted by 31 January. A further £100 is due for any return still outstanding 6 months later. It should be noted that the fixed penalties cannot exceed the amount that remains outstanding at the return due date.

Finally, there are also variable penalties HMRC may levy on individuals, for example, for failing to keep records and documents needed to complete a tax return.

3.3   PAY AS YOU EARN (PAYE)

Most employees in the UK do not have to complete a self-assessment tax return, as their tax is collected via PAYE. This means their employer must deduct income tax and National Insurance contributions from their pay, and forward the relevant amounts to HMRC.

An employer will know the correct amount to deduct, as the HMRC allocates a PAYE code to each employee. This consists of:

- **A number**
  - This indicates the amount of tax free income (usually) the employee is entitled to.
  - The last figure is always removed, and so you have to multiply by ten to quantify the full 'tax free' amount.
- **A letter**
  - This indicates the type of personal allowance entitlement.
  - There are different letters used to denote the different types of allowances an individual may be entitled to. The most interesting is a 'K code', as that indicates the individual has no tax-free income – the number given representing additional notional income.

EXAMPLE

A PAYE code of 512L equates to an annual tax-free income of £5,120, one-twelfth of which would be treated as non-taxable income by an employer each month. The 'L' in the code is the most common, as it represents those eligible for the basic personal allowance.

The PAYE system covers many payments including:

- Wages and salaries;
- Fees;
- Bonuses and commissions;
- Holiday pay;
- Pensions;
- Payments under profit sharing schemes;
- Statutory Sick Pay, Statutory Maternity Pay, Statutory Paternity Pay, Statutory Adoption Pay.

3.4 DEDUCTION AT SOURCE

The third method for HMRC to collect tax, is for the relevant amount to be deducted, at source, from savings and investments instruments and products. The rate deducted is always at the 'basic rate' for that particular instrument or product – if tax is to be reclaimed by a non-taxpayer, or additional tax is to be paid by a higher-rate taxpayer, the self assessment process is generally adopted.

The two most likely forms of income where you will be asked to calculate an income tax liability in the exam, are interest and dividend payments. Once you are comfortable with the procedure for both, you can apply the same rules across most of the other financial instruments and products (see Chapter 5 of this module).

- For **interest payments** (savings income), tax is normally deduced at source at **20%.**
- **Dividend payments** (dividend income) are paid net of a **10%** tax credit. (Unlike interest payments, the amount of this tax credit is notional and it is not physically paid to HMRC). Higher rate tax payers pay tax on dividends at 27.5%.

Collective investments are categorised as being liable to deduction of tax at source at 'savings rates' or 'dividend rates' depending on the nature of the asset class mix. For example, a unit trust consisting primarily of cash or fixed interest investments will have tax deducted at source at the savings rate of 20%. A different unit trust could have the majority of the investment in equities and therefore have tax effectively levied at source at 10%. There is more detail about this in Chapter 5 of this module.

3.4.1 Individual Liabilities

Despite the different rates of tax being deducted automatically at source, an individual is still taxed on their overall personal situation. As a result, it may be possible to reclaim tax paid at source, or it is equally possible that more tax may be due. This is probably information you are very comfortable with, but the table below highlights the key points:

	Savings income	Dividend income
Non- taxpayer	• Can reclaim the 20% deducted at source via self-assessment. • Interest payments can be paid gross if a saver completes an R85 form.	• Cannot reclaim any tax deducted at source.
Starter-rate taxpayer	• Can reclaim 10% of the amount deducted at source.	• Not applicable.
Basic-rate taxpayer	• No further liability.	• No further liability.
Higher-rate taxpayer	• Additional liability of 20% of the gross payment. (20%+20% = 40%).	• Additional liability of 22.5% of the gross payment. (10% + 22.5% = 32.5%).
Additional rate taxpayer	• Additional liability of 25% of the gross payment. (20% + 25% = 45%).	• Additional liability of 27.5% of the gross payment. (10% + 27.5% = 37.5%).

We will see more about how this works in practice, when looking at the income tax calculation.

3.5   INCOME TAX CALCULATION

Now we have looked at how tax is collected, we will concentrate on calculating an income tax liability. In the PCIAMs exam you are required to meet the objective of being able to calculate 'simple' tax computations.

There are six steps to an income tax calculation.

 Before looking at the six steps listed below, what do you think they involve, and in what order?

I	Calculate an individual's gross income for the year.
2	Deduct certain allowable amounts from the gross income.
3	Deduct personal allowances.
4	Calculate the amount of any payments for which higher-rate tax relief is given.
5	Tax the remaining income at the appropriate rates.
6	Give credit for any tax paid at source, and deduct any tax reducers.

We will look in more detail at each step, and incorporate the following case study as we work our way through each step.

CASE STUDY

Sandra Evans, aged 62, earns £46,000 per year, and 5% of that is deducted by her employer as a pension contribution. She also pays £300 per month into a personal pension plan.

She no longer has a company car, but her company provides her with private medical insurance, which has a taxable value of £800.

In 2013–14 her portfolio is expected to produce £1,800 interest net of tax and £2,700 net dividends.

3.5.1   Step 1: Calculate the gross income

There are two key Acts that lay down the rules for taxing different types of income:

*   Income Tax (Earnings and Pensions) Act 2003 – the 'ITEPA 2003';
*   Income Tax (Trading & Other Income) Act 2005 – the 'ITTOIA 2005'.

These effectively replaced the previous system of tax 'schedules'. Simplistically, most of the types of income that were covered under the old 'Schedule D' are now covered by the ITTOIA, with that of the old 'Schedule E' being covered by the ITEPA.

To calculate the gross income, we need to go back to Section 3.4.1, which concentrated on tax that was deducted at source on interest and dividend payments. We now need to 'gross up' these forms of income and add the result to the individual's other income.

Grossing up is a fairly straightforward process. For interest payments, you can gross up by dividing the net payment by 0.8 (ie, reversing the original process where the gross interest would have been multiplied by 0.8 (or 80%) to arrive at the net figure).

Based on this approach, for dividend payments you can gross up by dividing the net payment by 0.9.

CASE STUDY

Sandra has gross earnings of £46,000. In addition she is expecting:

*   Interest of £1,800. £1,800 ÷ 0.8 = £2,250

*   Dividends of £2,700. £2,700 ÷ 0.9 = £3,000

Sandra's expected gross income for 2013–14 is therefore £46,000 + £2,250 + £3,000 = **£51,250**

3.5.2   Step 2: Deduct certain allowable amounts

HMRC allow certain 'allowable amounts' to be deducted from gross income, before tax is applied. Possibly the best known of these, are pension contributions paid under the 'net pay' arrangement, for example personal contributions to company schemes.

To continue the pension theme, contributions to old style Retirement Annuity Contracts (RACs) can also be deducted here. These are still paid gross, mainly due to most pension providers running their RACs on out-dated computer platforms that are hard to convert to the more modern system for an investor to receive basic rate tax relief at source.

Other examples of 'allowable amounts' are:

- Share purchase and loans to companies, involving loans to small 'close' companies or loans to buy shares in them.
- Partnership investment, where tax relief is available to a partner who pays interest on a loan used to benefit a partnership.
- Payment of inheritance tax, where interest is allowable if it is paid on a loan used to meet an IHT liability. The relief is restricted to one year from taking out the loan.

CASE STUDY

Sandra's employer deducts 5% as a pension contribution. This equates to:

- **£46,000 x 5% = £2,300**

This is an allowable deduction from Sandra's gross income of £51,250, to leave £48,950.

Of this gross income, Sandra's non-savings income is £43,700 (£46,000 – £2,300). This is significant later.

3.5.3   Step 3: Deduct personal allowances

All UK residents, regardless of age (yes, this does include a new born baby), are eligible for the basic personal allowance. In 2013–14, this allowance is £9,440. Although we are all entitled to this amount, not all of us have a tax code of 944L, mainly due to enjoying 'benefits in kind' which are given a taxable value that is deducted from the standard personal allowance.

There are other personal allowances that could apply at this stage, such as the Blind Person's Allowance for those who are registered blind. The most common additional allowance that applies here, however, is the 'Age Allowance' for individuals who were already aged 65 by 5 April 2013.

For these individuals, their personal allowance is £10,500 in 2013–14 for those born between 6 April 1938 and 6 April 1948, and to £10,660 for those born before 6 April 1938. However, the increased amount is reduced by £1 for every £2 of income above a set statutory amount which is £26,100 in 2013–14. This reduction, if applicable, will not reduce the standard personal allowance, just the age allowance addition. It could also reduce the Married Couples Allowance (see Step 6).

For those born between 6 April 1938 and 6 April 1948, this effectively creates an additional tax band at 30% for income between £26,100 and £28,220, and for those aged 75 and over for income between £26,100 and £28,540. As far as possible, this should be avoided by investing in tax efficient investments, such as ISAs or National Savings Certificates, or life assurance bonds where tax on withdrawals can be delayed.

Similarly, from 2013–14 the standard personal allowance is reduced by £1 for each £2 of income in excess of £100,000, until it is eliminated entirely.

CASE STUDY

At age 62, Sandra is entitled to the basic personal allowance of £9,440. However, this will be reduced by £800 to take her taxable benefit-in-kind into account. Her taxable income will therefore be:

- **£48,950 – (£9,440 – £800) = £40,310**

Although this is the correct calculation for the taxable income, a good habit to get into, is to take the personal allowance off the non-savings income first. This is due to the order income is taxed, which is explained more in Step 5.

Sandra's non-savings income is £43,700 (the original £46,000 less the pension contribution of £2,300). Her revised personal allowance of £8,640 would therefore be taken off this to reach the amount of £35,060. The other income amounts of £2,250 (interest) and £3,000 (dividends) are added to this to arrive at the total taxable income amount of £43,275, as above.

3.5.4   Step 4: Calculate any amounts where higher rate relief is given

There are two primary situations where this happens, and they work in the same way. The two situations are:

- contributions to pensions plans, where basic rate tax relief is given at source, and
- gift aid contributions to charities.

If an individual makes these contributions during a tax year, the amount paid should be grossed up (by dividing by 0.8). The gross amount is then added to the statutory limit where taxable income is taxed at the basic rate (which in 2013–14 is £32,010).

The effect is that more of the individual's other income will be taxed at the basic rate rather than the higher rate, therefore effectively providing 'higher-rate tax relief'.

CASE STUDY

Sandra is paying £300 pm to a personal pension plan. This means a gross contribution of £375 (£300/0.8) is being invested on her behalf each month.

For this stage of the income tax calculation, we can extend the basic-rate tax band for her by:

- **£375 x 12 = £4,500**

Sandra's basic-rate band will therefore be extended to £36,510.

3.5.5   Step 5: Tax the income

We've finally reached the point where the taxable income is taxed! It is important that the income is taxed in the correct order and at the correct rate.

The correct order for the tax calculation is always:

1. earned income, then
2. savings income, then
3. dividend income, and finally
4. chargeable gains on life assurance policies.

The correct rates are:

	Non-taxpayers	Starting-rate taxpayers	Basic-rate taxpayers	Higher-rate taxpayers	Additional-rate taxpayers
Non-savings income	0%	N/A	20%	40%	45%
Savings income	0%	10%*	20%	40%	45%
Dividend income	10%	N/A	10%	32.5%	37.5%
Chargeable gains on life assurance policies	0% (20% tax paid in fund, non-reclaimable)	N/A	0% (20% tax paid in fund)	20%	25%

* The starting-rate of 10% to savings income only applies if there is insufficient non-savings income for the starting-rate band (£2,790 for tax year 2013–14) not to be exceeded.

In Step 3 we established that it was a good idea to deduct the personal allowance from the non-savings income. That is because the order in which income is taxed, is also the order in which allowances are deducted (ie, from non-savings income first, then savings income etc).

CASE STUDY

We have established that Sandra has an increased basic-rate band of £40,400. This leads to the following computation:

Type of income	Amount	Tax rate	Tax due
Non-savings income	£35,060	All at 20%	£7,002.00
Savings income	£1,450	All at 20%	£290.00
	£800	At 40%	£320.00
Dividend income	£3,000	All at 32.5%	£975.00
	£40,310		£8,597.00

Just to clarify, if Sandra hadn't been paying the personal pension contributions, she would have had the standard basic-rate band of £32,010. As a result, £4,500 more of her non-savings income would have been taxed at 40%. However, her £300 pm personal pension plan contribution translates to a gross annual payment of £4,500 and therefore an increased basic rate band, leaving less income taxed at the higher rate.

3.5.6   Step 6: Give credit for tax paid at source and deduct tax reducers

The previous steps of the process have established the total tax liability. However, we should take into account the fact that many individuals would have paid tax at source on their savings and dividend income. Therefore, to establish their **additional** tax liability, we should deduct these amounts.

We should also consider whether the individual could benefit from any tax reducers. These are simply amounts that can be deducted from the final tax bill. The common examples are:

- **Married couple allowance (MCA)**
  - This is now only available if either spouse (or civil partner) was born before 6 April 1935.
  - It provides relief at 10% of a fixed statutory amount that is updated each tax year ((£7915 for 2013–14 if older spouse in born before 6 April 1935).
  - For couples married before 5 December 2005, the MCA belongs to the husband, although it can be transferred to the wife.
  - For couples married or registered on or after 5 December 2005, the MCA is allocated to the higher earner. Couples subject to the old rules can elect for these new rules to apply to them.
- **Enterprise Investments Schemes (EIS)**
  - An investment in an EIS attracts tax relief at 30% of any contribution paid, up to a limit of £1,000,000 per tax year.
- **Venture Capital Trusts (VCTs)**
  - An investment in a VCT attracts tax relief at 30% of any contribution paid, up to a limit of £200,000 per tax year.

CASE STUDY

We have established that £8,597.00 is the expected **total** tax liability for Sandra. However, that includes tax on interest and dividends where she has already paid some tax at source.

The amounts paid at source were:

- Interest: £2,250 x 20% = £450

- Dividends: £3,000 x 10% = £300

Therefore, the **additional** tax Sandra will have to pay is:

- £8,597.00 – £450 – £300 = **£7,847.00**

She is not eligible for any tax reducers.

4.   CAPITAL GAINS TAX (CGT)

4.1   DEFINITION

Capital gains tax (CGT) is a tax on gains arising from the disposal of certain capital assets. We will look at what constitutes 'gains' later, but will start by defining disposals and chargeable assets.

4.1.1   Disposals

The most common disposal for CGT purposes is the sale of a chargeable asset. However, there are other examples of disposals that could give rise to a CGT liability, such as:

- gifting an asset;
- exchanges of property;
- loss or destruction of an asset (personal injury claims are specifically exempt);
- a capital sum received for a surrender of rights.

4.1.2   Exempt Assets

Chargeable assets for CGT are harder to define. Indeed, the easiest approach is to list some of the key **exempt assets**, in other words those that **do not** create a CGT liability on disposal. The main ones for our purposes are:

- an individual's principal private residence;
- private motor vehicles;
- gilts and most corporate bonds (excluding convertibles);
- assets held in ISAs and CTFs;
- most life policies, when in the hands of the original owner;
- National Savings Certificates and Premium Bonds;
- chattels (tangible moveable objects) where the value at disposal does not exceed £6,000;
- a chattel which is deemed a 'wasting asset' (basically, an expected life of less than 50 years);
- betting and lottery winnings;
- foreign currency, when for own personal use outside the UK;
- shares in VCTs;
- shares in EISs, as long as they have been held for at least three years;
- personal injury compensation.

In addition to the above, most UK residents are allowed use of an 'annual exemption' which, in 2013–14, covers the first £10,900 of gains. This is a 'use it or lose it' exemption, meaning that no unused element of the exemption from one tax year can be carried forward to the next tax year.

Chargeable Assets: property, land, buildings, leases, shares and investments, antiques, jewellery, possessions of more than £6,000 in value, business assets such as premises, goodwill and trademarks.

4.2   CGT CALCULATION

Just as we saw for the income tax calculation, there are now six steps to the CGT calculation. This has been simplified in recent years by the removal of indexation and tapering relief and the introduction of a flat rate of CGT, and so the calculation is a couple of steps shorter than it used to be!

Again, before looking at the six steps listed below, what do you think they involve and what is the correct order for calculating a possible CGT liability?

1	Determine the disposal proceeds.
2	Deduct the acquisition cost.
3	Deduct any purchase and sale costs, and any enhancement costs incurred.
4	Set off any allowable losses.
5	Deduct the annual exemption.
6	Calculate the tax at a flat rate of 18% or 28% if income subject to higher rate tax.

Again, we will look in more detail at each step, and incorporate the following case study as we work our way through each step.

CASE STUDY

Jon Carter, aged 46, earns £80,000 per year. In August 2013 he sold a holiday home that he purchased in 2001. The sale price was £245,000, and the purchase price £140,000.

Jon has kept all of his paperwork and has calculated the total cost of the purchase in 2001 was £2,600. The costs involved with the sale have amounted to £3,800.

During his time as owner of the property, Jon spent £21,000 on an extension in 2004. He also calculates that he spent £10,000 over the years maintaining the property to a good standard.

Jon has other investments, some of which have performed poorly. He sold some shares in November 2012, making a loss of £12,000. He has also sold units in a unit trust, incurring a loss of £4,300.

4.2.1   Step 1: Determine the disposal proceeds

The amount treated as the disposal proceeds is usually simply the sale proceeds. However, HMRC have to be satisfied that the sale is on a fully commercial basis. If it might not be, the market value of the asset at the time of the disposal will be used.

The 'market value' approach will be used when the disposal is not deemed to be at 'arms length'. This mainly occurs on two occasions, namely:

* a disposal between individuals with a close connection (ie, close relatives), and
* a disposal that is deliberately at undervalue or a gift between friends. The parties do not have to have a close connection in this situation, for the market value to be used.

CASE STUDY

Jon sold the property on the open market and received a fair commercial price. The disposal proceeds are therefore set at £245,000.

Disposal proceeds	Acquisition cost	Other costs	Losses	Annual exemption	Gain to be taxed
£245,000					

4.2.2 Step 2: Deduct the acquisition cost

The acquisition cost is usually the purchase price, as long as the asset was purchased on a commercial basis. If not, the above rules about 'market value' apply.

If the asset was acquired as a gift, the market value at the time of the gift is used.

An important date to remember for CGT purposes is 31 March 1982. This was when, in a previous regime, the value of all assets was rebased. Therefore, where an asset was acquired before 1 April 1982, the asset's cost is deemed to be the market value at 31 March 1982.

CASE STUDY

Jon also purchased the property on the open market and paid a fair commercial price. His purchase was after 31 March 1982 The acquisition cost is therefore set at £140,000.

Disposal proceeds	Acquisition cost	Other costs	Losses	Annual exemption	Gain to be taxed
£245,000	(£140,000)				

4.2.3 Step 3: Deduct any costs incurred when purchasing and selling

Incidental costs involved in the purchase and sale of an asset (such as legal fees, estate agent fees, stamp duty, auctioneer's fees etc) are deductible.

Costs involved in **enhancing** the asset (but not general maintenance) can also be deducted.

Note that no deductions are allowed for incidental costs of acquisition or enhancement expenditure before 31 March 1982, when values were re-based.

CASE STUDY

Jon can deduct the £2,600 cost on purchase, the £3,800 cost on sale and the £21,000 cost of the extension. He cannot deduct the £10,000 maintenance cost.

The total deduction at this stage is therefore: £2,600 + £3,800 + £21,000 = £27,400

Disposal proceeds	Acquisition cost	Other costs	Losses	Annual exemption	Gain to be taxed
£245,000	(£140,000)	(£27,400)			

4.2.4 Step 4: Set off any allowable capital losses

Losses incurred can be offset against gains made. Initially, a loss must be set off fully against any gains made in the same tax year. This is the case even if the subsequent overall gain is reduced to a figure below the annual exemption amount for that tax year.

If the gains are insufficient to absorb the loss, the remaining loss can be carried forward to subsequent years until it is fully used. There is no time limit for this carrying forward – it is indefinite. When offsetting a loss against a gain in a different tax year, it would only be necessary to use sufficient losses to reduce the gain to the annual exemption amount.

Losses brought forward from 1996–97 onwards must be used before losses brought forward from earlier years.

Losses on disposal of exempt assets cannot be offset against gains.

CASE STUDY

Jon has made a loss of £4,300 in this tax year, which must be offset against the gain he has made this tax year. He then has the choice as to whether he wants to use the £12,000 loss made in 2012–13, although given the amount of gain he made on the sale of the holiday home it is likely he will.

Disposal proceeds	Acquisition cost	Other costs	Losses	Annual exemption	Gain to be taxed
£245,000	(£140,000)	(£27,400)	(£16,300)		

4.2.5 Step 5: Deduct the annual exemption

In tax year 2013–14, the annual exemption is £10,900. It should be noted that this cannot be transferred between spouses.

The annual exemption that trustees are entitled to is half that allowed to individuals, so is £5,050 in 2013–14.

CASE STUDY

Jon will use the annual exemption to bring his gains down to the minimum.

Disposal proceeds	Acquisition cost	Other costs	Losses	Annual exemption	Gain to be taxed
£245,000	(£140,000)	(£27,400)	(£16,300)	(£10,900)	**£50,400**

4.2.6   Step 6: Tax the gain

From tax year 2011–12, capital gains have been taxed at 18% corresponding to basic rate income tax or 28% for higher and additional rate income tax bands.

1. See how much of the basic rate band is already being used against your taxable income.
2. Allocate any remaining basic rate band first against gains that qualify for Entrepreneurs' Relief – these are charged at 10%.
3. Next allocate any remaining basic rate band against your other gains; these are charged at 18%.
4. Any remaining gains above the basic rate band are charged at 28%.

CASE STUDY

Jon Carter is a higher rate income tax payer, so the 28% CGT rate will be used.

The gain to be taxed is £50,400 x 28% = £14,112.

So, from the sale of Jon's holiday home for £245,000, he stands to pay a CGT bill of £14,112.

4.3   PAYMENT OF CGT

As we mentioned in Chapter 3, capital gains are reported to HMRC as part of the self-assessment system.

Returning to the case study of Jon Carter that we have just used to illustrate the CGT calculation process, he sold the holiday home in August 2013. What do you think is the deadline for his capital gain of £14,112 to be paid to HMRC?

Any CGT payable is due on 31 January following the end of the tax year in which the gain was made. As a result, Jon is due to pay the CGT liability by 31 January 2015.

4.4   ADDITIONAL INFORMATION

This next section covers some of the CGT related information that you may need to be aware of.

4.4.1 Interspouse (and Inter-Civil Partner) Transactions

As the value of assets gets re-based on disposal, it is tempting for couples, married or registered, to swap the ownership between them on a regular basis, thereby minimising any potential gains in the value of the asset. This temptation has been recognised by HMRC and, as a result, there are special rules for disposals between spouses or civil partners.

A disposal from one spouse to another does NOT give rise to a chargeable gain, unless the disposal takes place after the tax year of separation but before divorce (in which case the 'market value' rule mentioned earlier would apply).

When the asset is eventually disposed of by the receiving spouse, the tax liability is based on the acquisition cost incurred by the first spouse. The transfer between spouses is known as a 'no gain no loss' disposal.

This facility can be used to transfer assets from a higher-rate taxpaying spouse to a lower-rate taxpaying spouse. (18%) The facility can also be used as a tax planning opportunity, by ensuring that both spouses fully use both annual exemptions before paying any CGT between them.

4.4.2 CGT on Death

There is no CGT on the disposal of assets following the death of an individual. The beneficiaries are deemed to acquire the assets at the market value at the date of death.

4.4.3 Chattels

Chattels are tangible moveable property, such as furniture. We noted earlier that these are exempt from CGT if the value (not the gain) at disposal does not exceed £6,000.

Chattels sold for more than £6,000 are therefore not exempt from CGT. However, it is possible to limit the gain to 5/3 x (Sale Price – £6,000) if the result of this calculation is less than the actual gain.

 Dominic purchased a painting for £1,000, and later he sold it for £9,000. What gain is assumed, for CGT purposes?

Using the above equation leads us to:

- 5/3 x (£9,000 – £6,000);
- 5/3 x (£3,000) = £5,000;
- As this is less than the actual gain of £8,000, this amount can be used by Dominic.

4.4.4 People with Multiple Homes

Just to clarify, individuals can elect which of their residences is to be treated as their 'main residence' and therefore be exempt from CGT. The election must be made within two years of the acquisition of the additional residence. If no election is made, HMRC can decide which property should be treated as the main residence.

Married couples (or civil partners) who are living together can only claim the exemption for one of their properties.

4.4.5   Shares

Shares of the same type and class can be purchased at different times, creating issues for determining the order of purchase and acquisitions.

Disposals of shares, or indeed of units in unit trusts, are identified with acquisitions in the following order:

- acquisitions on the same day;
- acquisitions within the following 30 days (preventing the use of 'bed and breakfasting');
- acquisitions in the share pool (which aggregates all other acquisitions not covered above. The average share price of the shares in the pool will be used).

EXAMPLE

Julie has a shareholding in **ABC plc**, which she acquired as follows:

- **6,000 shares on 2 September 1998 purchased for £5,000**

- **4,000 shares on 26 May 2002 purchased for £4,200**

- **2,000 shares on 22 July 2013 purchased for £1,400**

Following some bad news that impacted on the non-systematic risk of the share (see Module 7), Julie had sold 8,000 shares on 1 July 2013 for £2,800.

The sale and repurchase in July 2013 are grouped together:

- **Proceeds (£2,800 x 2,000 / 8,000)**   =   **£700**
- **Cost**   =   **(£1,400)**

                                                 –£700

Share pool

- **Proceeds (£2,800 x 6,000 / 8,000)**   =   **£2,100**
- **Cost (see below)**   =   **(£5,520)**

                                                 –£3,420

Chargeable loss   **–£4,120**

Share pool

	Number	Cost
		£
Purchase 2/9/98	6,000	5,000
Purchase 26/5/02	4,000	4,200
	10,000	9,200
Disposal 01/07/13 (9,200 x 6,000/10,000)	(6,000)	(5,520)
Balance carried forward	4,000	3,680

In this case, Julie has a chargeable loss to set against gains, of £4,120.

4.4.6   Shares of Negligible Value

There are occasions where share prices fall so far that they are deemed to have a 'negligible value'. In these situations, HMRC will treat these shares as being disposed of, despite the fact that they haven't physically been sold. This will allow an investor to crystallise a loss.

HMRC publishes a list of shares which it accepts have become of negligible value (www.hmrc.gov.uk/cgt/negvalist.htm). This includes some old investment trusts, a few football clubs and some well-known companies such as Land of Leather, Marconi and Northern Rock.

4.5   CGT RELIEFS

These are different to CGT exemptions in that a gain may be wholly or partly relieved against CGT.

4.5.1   Entrepreneur's Relief

This was introduced in April 2008 to replace business taper relief.

It can be claimed when an individual disposes of a business, or part of a business. The relief covers the qualifying gains that an individual makes during their lifetime.

For 2010–11 the relief was £2 million up to 22 June; but from 23 June it increased to £5 million. From 5 April 2011 the figure has been £10 million. This brings the rate of CGT down from 28% for higher-rate taxpayers to 10%.

Qualifying gains are:

- a disposal of the whole or part of a business run as a sole trader;
- the disposal of shares in a trading company, where the individual has at least a 5% shareholding and is also an employee of the company;
- the disposal of a share in a partnership by a partner.

The 'asset' must have been owned for at least one year before disposal.

4.5.2   Business Rollover Relief

This is a form of CGT deferral, which can be claimed by both incorporated and unincorporated businesses when they sell assets used in the business and buy other assets for the business.

There are a number of conditions for this relief to be available, including:

- the business must be trading, and
- the new assets must be purchased in a period starting one year before, and ending three years after, the disposal of the old assets.

This relief allows a business to expand, for example, into new (possibly larger) premises before selling their existing property, and defer the CGT from the sale of their existing property.

4.5.3   Reinvestment Relief into EIS Shares

This relief works along similar lines to Business Rollover Relief.

It is used by investors when making a gain on the disposal of an asset. If they invest that gain into shares that qualify under the Enterprise Investment Scheme, the CGT is deferred.

As with Business Rollover Relief, the investment must be made in a period starting one year before, and ending three years after, the disposal of the asset subject to CGT.

4.5.4   Holdover Relief

This is effectively a form of CGT deferral again, being able to 'hold over' the gain on gifts of certain assets. When this relief is claimed, no CGT becomes payable at the time of the gift, but the acquisition cost to the receiver (the donee) of the gift is reduced by the amount of held-over gain.

This relief can only be given if both the donor and donee jointly claim it, and the donee is resident and ordinarily resident in the UK (see Chapter 2 of this module for details, if needed).

The relief is available on gifts of trading assets, which are:

*   assets used in the trade of the donor by the donor's personal company;
*   shares and securities of trading companies, provided they are not quoted on a recognised stock exchange or they are those of the donor's personal company (ie, the donor has at least 5% of the voting rights).

Holdover relief is also available on transfers to trusts that attract an immediate charge to IHT (Chargeable Lifetime Transfers – more of which in Chapter 6 of this module).

5.   TAXATION OF INVESTMENT VEHICLES

5.1   INTRODUCTION

In the previous two chapter of this module we have looked at the basics of income tax and capital gains tax. In this module we will relate how these taxes impact on the major investment products and vehicles, both from the liability for the investor and also the liability incurred within the investment vehicle/product.

This will not be a detailed explanation of each product, as that is covered in more detail in Module 5 'Financial Instruments and Products'. We will stick to just the taxation aspects, using a similar format throughout to help you compare each (where possible). The format we will follow is this:

	Income Tax	Capital Gains Tax
Tax situation of the product		
Tax situation for the investor		
Other details of note:		

Throughout the explanations:

- 'TP' stands for taxpayer;
- 'SRTP' stands for starter-rate taxpayer;
- 'BRTP' stands for basic-rate taxpayer;
- 'HRTP' stands for higher-rate taxpayer;
- 'ARTP' stands for additional-rate taxpayer.

5.1.1   Bank and Building Society Savings Accounts

	Income Tax	**Capital Gains Tax**
Tax situation of the product	20% taken at source (savings income)	N/A
Tax situation for the investor	• Non-TP may reclaim 20% • SRTP may reclaim 10% • BRTP has no further liability • HRTP has a further liability of 20% of the gross interest • ARTP has a further liability of 25% of the gross interest	• N/A (the only return received is income, there are no capital gains)
Other details of note: A non-TP may avoid having to reclaim the 20% taken at source by completing an R85 form, which enables the provider to credit gross interest.		

5.1.2   National Savings and Investments

This product group is a bit more complicated, as NS&I operate different products with different tax implications.

Tax free products	**Products taxed at 20% at source (with no further liability for SRTP or BRTP)**	**Products that are taxable but paid / credited in full (without deduction of tax at source)**
• Direct ISA	• Guaranteed Growth Bonds	• Income Bonds
• Cash ISA	• Guaranteed Income Bonds	• Investment Account
• Premium Bonds		• Easy Access Savings Account
• Fixed interest savings certificates		• Direct Saver
• Index-linked savings certificates		
• Children's Bonus Bonds		

5.1.3 Government Gilts

	Income Tax	Capital Gains Tax
Tax situation of the product	• Income (savings income) normally paid gross (since April 1998)	N/A
Tax situation for the investor	• Non-TP has no further action to take • SRTP has a 10% liability • BRTP has a 20% liability • HRTP has a 40% liability • ARTP has a 50% liability	• Gilts are exempt from CGT

Other details of note: Any accrued interest on the sale proceeds of gilts is liable to income tax if the individual's total nominal holding of gilts exceeds £5,000. Also exempt from stamp duty.

5.1.4 Corporate Bonds

	Income Tax	Capital Gains Tax
Tax situation of the product	• Income paid net of 20% (savings income)	**N/A**
Tax situation for the investor	• Non-TP may reclaim • SRTP may reclaim 10% • BRTP has no further liability • HRTP has a further liability of 20% of the gross coupon (interest) payment • ARTP has a further liability of 25% of the gross coupon	• Some corporate bonds are exempt from CGT (ie, if they meet the definition of a 'qualifying corporate bond') • If exempt, profits are tax free, but losses are not allowable • Most bonds issued by companies on or after 1 April 1996 will be 'qualifying' due to new rules introduced in the Finance Act 1996, including relevant discounted securities, but not convertibles.

Other details of note: Some corporate bonds are issued as 'deeply discounted securities', where the issue price is less than the amount payable on redemption, by more than 15% or more than 0.5% per year. Profits on the disposal or redemption of these securities will be taxed as income, as opposed to a capital gains.

5.1.5 Company Shares

	Income Tax	**Capital Gains Tax**
Tax situation of the product	• Income paid with a tax credit of 10% (dividend income)	N/A
Tax situation for the investor	• Non-TP cannot reclaim • BRTP has no further liability • HRTP has a further liability of 22.5% of the grossed-up dividend • ARTP has a further liability of 27.5% of the grossed-up dividend	• Liable for CGT • See Sections 4.4.5 and 4.4.6 for details
Other details of note:		

5.1.6 Investment Trusts

	Income Tax	**Capital Gains Tax**
Tax situation of the product	• Income paid with a tax credit of 10% (dividend income)	• Exempt on disposals made within the investment trust
Tax situation for the investor	• Non-TP cannot reclaim • BRTP has no further liability • HRTP has a further liability of 22.5% of the grossed-up dividend • ARTP has a further liability of 27.5% of the grossed-up dividend	• Liable for CGT • See Sections 4.4.5 and 4.4.6 for details
Other details of note:		

5.1.7   Unit Trusts and OEICs

The tax situation of these collective products depends on the asset make-up of the products.

If at least 60% of the assets are interest-bearing:

	Income Tax	Capital Gains Tax
Tax situation of the product	• 20% taken at source (savings income)	• Exempt
Tax situation for the investor	• Non-TP may reclaim • SRTP may reclaim 10% • BRTP has no further liability • HRTP has a further liability of 20% of the gross interest • ARTP has a further liability of 25% of the gross interest	• There is a CGT liability on disposal (despite the fact the underlying assets may be CGT free or exempt)
Other details of note:		

If less than 60% of the assets are interest-bearing:

	Income Tax	Capital Gains Tax
Tax situation of the product	• Income paid with a tax credit of 10% (dividend income)	• Exempt
Tax situation for the investor	• Non-TP cannot reclaim • BRTP has no further liability • HRTP has a further liability of 22.5% of the grossed-up dividend • ARTP has a further liability of 27.5% of the grossed-up dividend	• Liable for CGT • See Sections 4.4.5 and 4.4.6 for details
Other details of note:		

5.1.8 Exchange Traded Funds (ETFs)

	Income Tax	Capital Gains Tax
Tax situation of the product	• Income paid with a tax credit of 10% (dividend income)	• Exempt
Tax situation for the investor	• Non-TP cannot reclaim • BRTP has no further liability • HRTP has a further liability of 22.5% of the gross dividend • ARTP has a further liability of 27.5% of the grossed-up dividend	• Liable for CGT
Other details of note: ETF's do not create a stamp duty charge on purchase.		

5.1.9 Individual Savings Accounts (ISAs and Junior ISAs)

An ISA isn't a product as such, but a tax wrapper that can be used to make an existing investment vehicle or product more tax efficient.

For Cash ISAs, refer to Section 5.1.1, where the investment vehicles currently incur an income tax liability. Attaching the ISA wrapper to these vehicles removes the income tax liability, making them tax-free.

For stocks and shares ISAs, refer to Sections 5.1.3–5.1.8, where there is currently an income tax and CGT liability for an investor. Attaching the ISA wrapper to these types of investment vehicles removes the CGT liability for the investors completely. The income tax liability is limited to the non-reclaimable 10% tax credit.

5.1.10 Child Trust Funds (CTFs)

	Income Tax	Capital Gains Tax
Tax situation of the product	• Savings accounts: Tax free • Shares and Stakeholder accounts: Income paid with a tax credit of 10% (dividend income)	• Exempt
Tax situation for the investor	• No further liability but tax credit can't be reclaimed	• Exempt
Other details of note: CTF's are exempt from the rule, which states a parent is taxable on a child's investment income of more than £100, if the capital came from the parent.		

5.1.11 Derivatives (Futures and Options)

	Income Tax	**Capital Gains Tax**
Tax situation of the product	• No income produced	• N/A
Tax situation for the investor	• No income produced	• Liable for CGT

Other details of note: In very rare circumstances, transactions may be treated by HMRC as a trading activity and therefore be liable to income tax.

If a tax avoidance scheme uses futures or options to produce a return that is effectively guaranteed, the profit is subject to income tax (under ITTOIA).

5.1.12 Enterprise Investment Scheme (EIS)

	Income Tax	**Capital Gains Tax**
Tax situation of the product	• Income paid with a tax credit of 10% (dividend income)	• N/A
Tax situation for the investor	• Non-TP cannot reclaim • BRTP has no further liability • HRTP has a further liability of 22.5% of the grossed-up dividend • ARTP has a further liability of 27.5% of the grossed-up dividend	• CGT free as long as shares held for three years • CGT deferral relief possible (see Section 4.5.3 for details)

Other details of note:

- Investment into an EIS receives tax relief at 30% (from April 2011) up to a maximum contribution of £1,000,000 per tax year. This relief is given as a tax reducer.
- Income tax relief is withdrawn if shares are disposed of within three years.
- It is possible to carry back investments to a previous tax year, to receive tax relief in that previous year (as long as the overall maximum limit of £500,000 is not exceeded).

5.1.13 Venture Capital Trusts (VCTs)

	Income Tax	Capital Gains Tax
Tax situation of the product	• Income paid with a tax credit of 10% (dividend income)	• Exempt
Tax situation for the investor	• Non-TP cannot reclaim • BRTP, HRTP and ARTP no further liability	• CGT free with no minimum holding period

Other details of note:

- Investments into a VCT receive tax relief at 30%, up to a maximum investment limit of £200,000 per tax year. This relief is given as a tax reducer.
- Income tax relief is withdrawn if shares are disposed of within five years.

5.1.14 Personal Pension Plans (PPPs)

	Income Tax	Capital Gains Tax
Tax situation of the product	• Income credited with a tax credit of 10% (dividend income)	• Exempt
Tax situation for the investor	• Any income taken from a pension fund is taxable at the individual's highest marginal rate	• Exempt

Other details of note:

- Contributions to a PPP benefit from tax relief at source, meaning a net investment made by an individual is grossed up immediately at the basic rate by the provider.
- Higher-rate tax relief is available by extending an individual's basic rate band by the gross contribution.
- 25% of the pension fund can be taken as a tax-free lump sum.

5.1.15 Qualifying Life Assurance Products

	Income Tax	Capital Gains Tax
Tax situation of the product	• Income paid within the fund (equivalent to 20% when combined with CGT)	• CGT paid within the fund (equivalent to 20% when combined with income tax)
Tax situation for the investor	• Non TP can't reclaim • BRTP has no further liability • HRTP has no further liability • ARTP has no further liability	• Exempt when in the hands of the original owner

Other details of note:

• There are a number of rules that check to see whether a life assurance plan is 'qualifying' or not. The most basic of these is that contributions must be paid at least annually, which clearly rules out single premium life assurance products.

5.1.16 Non-Qualifying Life Assurance Products

	Income Tax	Capital Gains Tax
Tax situation of the product	• Income paid within the fund (equivalent to 20% when combined with CGT)	• CGT paid within the fund (equivalent to 20% when combined with income tax)
Tax situation for the investor	• Non TP can't reclaim • BRTP has no further liability • HRTP has a further liability of 20% of the chargeable gain following a chargeable event • ARTP has a further liability of 25% of the chargeable gain	• Exempt when in the hands of the original owner

Other details of note:

- An investor is allowed to take annual payments of up to 5% of the original investment with no immediate liability to income tax, regardless of their tax status.
- This can be done for a maximum of 20 years (ie, effectively the investor is having their capital returned in chunks). However, the withdrawals do not have to be consistent as the allowance is cumulative, meaning an investor may be able to withdraw a lot more than 5% of the original investment if they have not taken any previous withdrawals.
- If an investor takes more than the 5% allowance, there may be a personal income tax liability if the gain, when added to their other income for the year, makes them a higher-rate taxpayer (remember Section 3.5.5 listing the order that income is taxed, with 'chargeable gains' the last item).
- When an investor cashes in their investment, a calculation is made to determine the chargeable gain and see if there is a further liability for the investor.
- In both of these situations, an investor who is still in the basic rate band can use 'top slicing' to help them remain in that band and create no further liability. Top slicing is of no use to an investor who is already a higher-rate taxpayer before the chargeable gain is added to their income.
- A simple comparison example of this process is given below.

TOP SLICING EXAMPLE

Bill and Ben are twins. Bill earns £30,000 pa after the deduction of his personal allowance, whereas Ben earns £31,110 pa after the deduction of his personal allowance. They both took out investment bonds 8.5 years ago, each investing £100,000.

They have both been taking 5% of this original investment at the start of each year as they have been told there would be no tax to pay on it immediately. The bonds are now both worth £67,000 and they have decided to encash them.

Bill	Ben
• Cash-in value £67,000	• Cash-in value £67,000
• Add withdrawals of 9 x £5,000 = £45,000	• Add withdrawals of 9 x £5000 = £45,000
• Less original investment (£100,000)	• Less original investment (£100,000)
• Chargeable gain = £12,000	• Chargeable gain = £12,000
• The gain has been made over eight full years and so can be 'sliced' by eight	• The gain has been made over eight full years and so can be 'sliced' by eight
• £12,000 ÷ 8 = £1,500 slice	• £12,000 ÷ 8 = £1,500 slice
• This is added to the top of Bill's taxable income for the year of £30,000, making a total income for the year of £31,500.	• This is added to the top of Ben's taxable income for the year of £31,110, making a total income for the year of £32,610.
• This is below the basic rate band for 2013–14 of £32,010 and so Bill has no further liability	• This is £600 above the basic rate band for 2013–14 of £32,010 and so this amount is taxed at an additional 20%
	• £600 x 20% = £120
	• We then need to multiply this back up by the number of full years the bond was in force for
	• £120 x 8 = £960
	• Ben will have an additional tax liability of £960 following the encashment of his bond

5.2 OVERSEAS INVESTMENTS

The main attraction of offshore products, many of which are available to UK investors, is that they are usually established in low-tax countries, so the investment should roll up more or less free of tax. This is known as 'gross roll-up'. However, this fact alone does not mean that an offshore product is automatically better than an onshore product.

5.2.1 Offshore Sterling Deposit Accounts

These are generally situated in tax havens such as the Channel Islands or the Isle of Man. They may pay higher interest rates than the equivalent onshore accounts and, significantly, they pay interest gross.

As we said in Chapter 2 of this module, UK resident taxpayers are taxed on the arising basis. As a result, whether the interest earned is brought into the UK or not, a UK resident is taxed at the same rate as on UK savings income: 10%; 20%; 40% or 45%.

There is no particular benefit for a UK resident to invest in offshore deposit accounts, except for non-taxpayers automatically receiving the interest gross.

5.2.2   Offshore Life Policies

These are issued in countries such as Luxembourg, the Republic of Ireland, the Channel Islands and the Isle of Man. As mentioned already, the perceived advantage is 'gross roll-up' due to the tax position of the fund. This could be a significant advantage over the long-term.

As all offshore policies issued after 17 November 1983 are deemed to be non-qualifying, the chargeable gain is fully assessed to tax at 20%, 40% or 45% following a chargeable event. Just as with onshore bonds, top slicing can be used to calculate the liability.

Time apportionment relief is available for periods of residence outside of the UK, based on the percentage time the investor was non-UK resident during the term of the policy. However, this still means that the whole of the gain is chargeable if the policyholder was a UK resident for the whole of the policy term.

A quick comparison of onshore and offshore bonds for a higher-rate taxpaying UK resident is therefore:

Onshore		Offshore	
Gain in fund	£100,000	Gain in fund	£100,000
Less tax at 20% in the fund	(£20,000)	Investor's tax at 40%	(£40,000)
Net gain	£80,000	**Net gain**	£60,000
Investor's additional tax at 20%	(£16,000)		
Net gain	**£64,000**		

Of course, the investor hopes that the tax efficient fund growth in the offshore bond will more than compensate for the difference in tax treatment.

5.2.3   Offshore Funds

Again, offshore funds are generally set up in territories where there is little or no tax, such as Luxembourg, the Republic of Ireland, the Channel Islands and the Isle of Man. They may be suitable for certain investors, in particular those who are non-UK resident, as offshore income and gains are free of tax.

For tax purposes, offshore funds are divided into distributor ('reporting') and non-distributor ('non-reporting') funds.

Dividends from **distributor funds** are treated as gross income, and taxed at the standard dividend rates of 10%, 32.5% or 37.5%. Gains from these funds are subject to CGT, with the calculation based on standard CGT principles and with the investor being able to use the CGT annual exemption to keep a gain to a minimum.

For **non-distributor funds**, the idea is that most income is accumulated and little or no dividends are paid. The gain on disposal is calculated using CGT principles, but the gain is actually liable to income tax (not CGT) at the investor's highest marginal rate. The CGT annual allowance cannot be used to limit this income tax liability.

Distributor funds are generally preferable for most UK investors due to the lower tax rates on dividends and the maximum 28% CGT rate on gains. Also, because the income is received gross, non-taxpayers benefit.

However, non-distributor funds do have the advantage of income being accumulated in a low tax environment and so the investment should grow faster. They are sometimes used by UK residents to roll up income and only realise the profits when they become non-UK resident.

6.   INHERITANCE TAX (IHT)

6.1   DEFINITION

Inheritance tax (IHT) is charged on certain transfers of property or 'value' – it is therefore not just a death duty!

The individual who makes the transfer is known as the donor (or transferor). The individual who receives the transfer is known as the donee (or transferee).

Going back to a topic we covered in Chapter 2 of this module, the concept of domicility is crucial for IHT liabilities.

 Thinking back, how does an individual's domicile status impact on their IHT liability?

Donors who are domiciled, or deemed domiciled, in the UK are subject to IHT on their worldwide property. Donors who are non-UK domiciled are subject to IHT on their UK property only.

6.2   IHT RATES

There are three rates of IHT, which are linked to the prevailing nil-rate band (NRB). In 2013–14 the NRB is £325,000. The rates are:

*   £0–£325,000   0% (for any cumulative value of transfers);
*   Over £325,000   20% (for chargeable lifetime transfers);
*   Over £325,000   40% (for transfers on or within seven years prior to death subject to taper relief).

If at least 10% of the deceased's estate is left to charity, a reduced rate of 36% applies.

6.3 TYPES OF TRANSFER

There are four types of transfer that a donor can make.

 Before looking at the answers below, what do you think these are?

The types of transfer are:

- exempt;
- potentially exempt;
- chargeable;
- transfers on death.

We will go on to look at each of these in more detail.

6.3.1 Exempt Transfers

These are simply transfers that are not taxed. The following table lists the main exempt transfers, along with relevant details and whether the transfer is exempt if made during the lifetime of the donor only, or during their lifetime and on their death.

Type	Monetary amount (if applicable)	Relevant details
Interspouse (and inter-civil partner)	• Unlimited if donee is a UK domicile • If donee is non-UK-domiciled in UK there are special rules which were changed in April 2013	• This exemption can be applied both during lifetime and on death. • Spouses have to be married and not 'common law'. • Transfers are exempt, even if the spouses no longer live with each other (different to CGT rules).
Annual exemption	• £3,000 per tax year	• This is just a lifetime exemption. • If the whole £3,000 is not used in a tax year, the balance can be carried forward for one year only.
Small gifts	• £250 to any person in any one tax year	• This is just a lifetime exemption. • It can be used a number of times, to different donees. • It **can't** be used in conjunction with the annual exemption as part of a larger gift.

Type	Monetary amount (if applicable)	Relevant details
Normal expenditure	• No limit	• This is just a lifetime exemption. • After making the gift, the donor should be able to maintain their ordinary standard of living. • The expenditure must be regular, or if the first in a series, clear evidence of an intention must be ongoing. • Payments must be made out of taxable income, not inheritances, lottery winnings, capital from share sales, proceeds from life assurance bonds.
Gifts on marriage/ civil partnership	• £5,000 from each parent • £2,500 from remoter ancestor • £2,500 from bride or groom • £1,000 from any other	• This is just a lifetime exemption.
Gifts for education & maintenance	• 'Reasonable provision'	• This is just a lifetime exemption. • Payments exempt until child's 18th birthday, or ending full time education (if later). • Illegitimate, step and adopted children included.
Gifts to charities & political parties	• Unlimited	• This exemption can be applied both during lifetime and on death.
Gifts for the national benefit	• Unlimited	• This exemption can be applied both during lifetime and on death. • Includes gifts to museums, libraries, universities, the National Trust and Housing associations
Death on active service	• Entire estate	• The estates of members of the armed forces are tax free, if they die because of wounds received or diseases contracted whilst on active service.

6.3.2 Potentially Exempt Transfers (PETs)

A PET is a lifetime transfer by a donor to:

- another individual;
- a bare trust;
- a disabled trust.

Up until 21 March 2006, transfers into interest in possession and accumulation & maintenance trusts were also treated as PETs. Since this date, they are now regarded as Chargeable Lifetime Transfers (see Section 6.3.3).

No tax is charged at the date of the PET, and the transfer does not even have to be reported to HMRC. If the donor survives seven years, the transfer becomes fully exempt and is excluded from any IHT calculation.

If the donor dies within seven years of making the transfer, the tax due can be tapered down based on how long the donor lived after making the transfer. The tapering table shown below is based on the tax due, not the value of the PET itself. The donee is liable to pay any tax due.

Years between transfer & death	Percentage of tax due
Up to 3	100%
More than 3 but not more than 4	80%
More than 4 but not more than 5	60%
More than 5 but not more than 6	40%
More than 6 but not more than 7	20%
More than 7	Exempt

 George gifted £100,000 to his daughter, Zoe, in April 2005, to help her buy her first house. He died in June 2010, leaving an estate of £500,000 which is split equally between George's five nephews. What is Zoe's IHT liability, if any, on the amount she received?

The answer is that she is not liable for any tax, as the gift falls below the NRB (and transfers are measured in chronological order, so the gift of £100,000 is the first amount set against the NRB). Of course, if George has survived another couple of years, the gift would have become exempt and would not be included in the IHT calculation at all.

It is important to note from this example that, although the tapering table was unused, there is still a possible advantage in that IHT is chargeable on the value of the PET at the date it was made, not the date of death effectively putting a ceiling in the value of the gift.

It is possible to use the value of the property transferred at the date of death, if it has fallen since the date of the original transfer. This rule does not apply to chattels deemed to be 'wasting assets' (ie, having a useful life of 50 years or less).

6.3.3 Chargeable Lifetime Transfers (CLTs)

These are transfers that are not exempt or potentially exempt. The most common transfers are lifetime gifts to trusts, other than to bare trusts and trusts for a disabled person (which we have already established are PETs) and transfers to a company.

Tax on CLTs is payable at 20% on the excess above the NRB at the time of the transfer with a further 20% payable on death. There will be no further tax to pay if the donor then survives seven years. If they don't, additional tax will be due, based on the higher death rate, although any tax already paid will be offset, and the same tapering table used for PETs can be utilised.

The rules that apply to PETs about the value of the transfer being based on the date of transfer and not the date of death, also apply to CLTs. In addition, the 'reduction in value' rule also applies.

6.3.4 Transfers on Death

IHT is chargeable on the death of an individual, with the tax chargeable as if the deceased had made a transfer of value equal to the value of his or her estate immediately before death. The taxable estate is the individual's assets, less their liabilities. These assets might include the value of life policies payable on the death of the individual.

There are also certain types of asset that are excluded, including:

*   assets situated outside the UK (for a non-UK domiciled individual);
*   unit trust and OEIC holdings where the beneficial owner is a non-UK domicile.

6.3.5 Gifts with Reservation

A Gift with Reservation is a gift which is not fully given away by the donor, so the donee either receives the gift with conditions attached, or the donor retains some benefit. Examples where this occurs include gifting the deeds of a house but continuing to live there without paying a market rent, or gifting the ownership of a work of art but still having the work in the donor's property.

The consequences of making a Gift with Reservation are not very tax-efficient and may, in fact, result in a double IHT charge. The 'gift' is treated as a transfer of value at the time it is made, which may be immediately chargeable or become chargeable on the death of the donor within seven years. However, the 'gift' never actually leaves the donor's estate and so, on their death, it is added back into the estate on the basis of its value at death.

An extension of this concept is that of Pre-Owned Assets Tax (POAT). This is an income tax charge on the benefit individuals receive by having free or low-cost enjoyment or use of certain assets they used to own, or provided the funds to purchase. This charge came into effect in April 2005, but can apply to such arrangements put in place, all the way back to March 1986.

By paying the POAT income tax charge, the individual avoids possible IHT on the transaction. It is therefore sometimes a tough judgement call to decide whether to elect for the asset involved to be subject to IHT on death by opting out of POAT, or to remain paying the POAT income tax charge.

6.4   CUMULATION PRINCIPLE

This is a crucial aspect that applies to the calculation of IHT, whether chargeable during a donor's lifetime or on death. As we have already seen, transfers that are potentially exempt remain in the IHT calculation process for seven years. If the cumulative value of all PETs exceeds the NRB on the donor's death IHT will be due on the excess. This is when the tapering relief comes into play, although it should be remembered that PETs are set against the NRB in chronological order so, conceivably, the PET that leads to the NRB being exceeded will be the most recent one and therefore the taper relief may be limited.

As far as CLTs are concerned, again all CLTs over a seven-year period are added together, with tax immediately payable once the NRB is exceeded.

A transfer drops out of the cumulation once it is more than seven years old. However, even transfers that have 'dropped out' may still be relevant for a PET made within seven years of the original transfer. This is one of the most complex areas applying to IHT and means that it is possible that CLTs made up to 14 years before a donor's death may be included in the cumulation process. There wouldn't be any tax to pay on these old CLTs themselves, but by being included in the cumulation it is more likely the estate will fall (partly or wholly) above the NRB and be liable to tax.

6.5   TRANSFER OF THE NRB

In October 2007, the Chancellor announced a change to the IHT process and how the NRB can be extended for married couples/people in civil partnerships. The change was based on the fact that the NRB on the first death was often wasted because all or most of the property was transferred to the surviving spouse/civil partner. These transfers would fall under the interspouse exemption anyway.

The ruling announced in October 2007 means that, as long as the second death occurred after 8th October 2007 (and the couple were married/in a civil partnership at the time of the first death) the percentage of any unused prevailing NRB can be carried forward and applied to the NRB at the time of the second death. This amount is then added to the standard prevailing NRB at the time of the second death.

It is probably easiest to see how this works, via an example.

EXAMPLE

Laurence and Anne were married in 1961. Laurence died in January 2002 when the NRB was £242,000. He left £60,500 to his son, and the remaining estate of £400,000 to Anne. She dies in June 2010 when the NRB is £325,000.

At the time of Laurence's death, 25% of the prevailing NRB was used by non-exempt transfers:

*   **£60,500 ÷ £242,000 x 100 = 25%**

This means that 75% was unused, as the remainder of the estate was passed under the interspouse exemption. Anne therefore 'inherited' this unused percentage.

As a result, on her death in 2013, her NRB is increased accordingly:

*   **£325,000 (NRB) x 75% = £243,750**

This is added to the standard NRB to make a total NRB for Anne on her death of:

*   **£325,000 + £243,750 = £568,750**

This increase applies, even if the surviving spouse (Anne in this case) had re-married by the time of her death. However, there is an upper limit of 100% by which the NRB can be increased, so the NRB can never be more than double that prevailing at the date of second death.

6.6   IHT TRANSACTIONS

We mentioned right at the start of this chapter that IHT is charged on certain transfers of property or 'value'. A 'transfer of value' is a reduction in the donor's estate. Therefore, an interest free loan that is repayable on demand or on death is not treated as a transfer of value. Neither is a commercial transaction where full consideration is received, even if this transaction was a 'bad bargain' (ie, not the best the individual could have negotiated). It should be noted that commercial transactions between family members or business partners are closely scrutinised to ensure they are truly commercial!

The 'loss to the estate' amount might not be the same as the actual value of a gift. An example commonly used, for some reason, is that of an individual owning two expensive vases. Together they may be worth £100,000, but individually they are only worth £20,000. If one vase is gifted away by a donor, the loss to the estate is not the £20,000 single value of the individual vase, but £80,000 as the estate is worth £80,000 less after the gift has been made.

The 'related property' rules are important here, as an individual's assets may be related to similar assets held by their spouse or civil partner. The rules ensure that, when measuring an individual's transfer of value for IHT purposes, account must be taken of these similar assets held by a spouse or civil partner as they are effectively treated as being one asset. This has particular relevance where spouses/civil partners own shares in the same unquoted company, as their joint shareholding is looked at to establish the extent of the loss to the estate on gifting shares away.

6.6.1   Interaction between IHT and CGT

There is considerable interaction between IHT and CGT.

A valuation for IHT is not always the same as a valuation for CGT, as for IHT it is the loss to the estate that is measured, whereas for CGT it is the asset that is valued. However, where an asset is valued for IHT on the death of an individual, the same value is used for CGT purposes. This is then treated as the beneficiary's acquisition cost.

If a disposal attracts an immediate charge to IHT, for example setting up a discretionary trust, CGT holdover relief can generally be claimed as discussed earlier in Chapter 4 (Section 4.5.4 of this module). Where no holdover relief is claimed, any IHT liability paid can be deducted when calculating the gain provided the IHT was paid by the donor.

No CGT holdover relief will be available for exempt or potentially exempt transfers.

Earlier, in Section 6.3.5, we talked about Gifts with Reservation, and their lack of effectiveness for IHT purposes. It should be noted that, although such gifts never leave the donor's estate as far as IHT is concerned, they would be regarded as being disposals of assets for CGT.

6.7   IHT RELIEFS

Just as we looked at reliefs that can apply to CGT, we will now briefly look at the reliefs that can apply to IHT. The three main ones we will look at are:

- quick succession relief;
- business property relief;
- agricultural property relief.

6.7.1   Quick Succession Relief (QSR)

QSR is available where property in the deceased's estate has passed to them by a chargeable transfer in the five years before their death. Therefore, the property has been valued for IHT purposes and QSR is an attempt to limit the same property being fully chargeable twice in quick succession.

The relief is given by reducing the tax payable on the deceased's estate, by referring to the amount of tax payable on the earlier chargeable transfer, the benefit that passed to the deceased on that transfer, and the period between the transfer and the death.

6.7.2   Business Property Relief (BPR)

This is a relief for transfers of business property, designed to try to ensure family businesses (for example) aren't crippled by having to pay an IHT bill.

BPR is claimed at two rates. The relief is **100%** for:

- interests in unincorporated businesses, such as sole traders or partnerships;
- shareholdings of any size in unquoted and Alternative Investment Market (AIM) companies.

The relief is 50% for:

- controlling shareholdings in fully listed companies;
- land, buildings, plant or machinery used wholly or mainly for the purpose of a business controlled by the donor (or if the donor was a partner).

BPR is only available if the donor owned the property for at least two years.

There are some assets that do not qualify for BPR, including:

- businesses that consist wholly, or mainly, of dealing in securities, stocks or shares, land or buildings, or making or holding investments;
- where the property concerned is subject to a binding contract for sale at the time of the transfer.

6.7.3   Agricultural Property Relief

This relief is available for the transfer during lifetime or death, of agricultural property in the UK, Channel Islands or Isle of Man. 'Agricultural property' includes agricultural land, growing crops and farm buildings, but not the animals or equipment. (A way to think of this is if you could pick up the land and turn it over, anything that doesn't fall, qualifies!)

Agricultural Property Relief is also claimed at two rates. The relief is 100% for:

- owner-occupied farms;
- land that was let on a grazing licence;
- property that is let on a tenancy beginning on or after 1 September 1995.

The relief is 50% for interests of landlords in most other let farmland.

The property must have been occupied by the donor for agricultural purposes for the previous two years, or have been owned by the donor for seven years and occupied by someone else for agricultural purposes for that time. As with BPR, the relief cannot apply to property that is subject to a binding contract for sale.

Where both Agricultural Property Relief and BPR are both available, Agricultural Property Relief is given first. Often assets in a farming business will qualify for BPR even if they didn't qualify for Agricultural Property Relief.

6.8   ADMINISTRATION OF ESTATES

The IHT payable on the estate of a deceased person is the liability of the legal personal representatives. The actual tax is due six months after the end of the month in which death occurs.

The quick settlement of IHT is important for the legal personal representatives, as they cannot obtain grant of representation to administer the estate, until they have accounted for the deceased's assets and paid the IHT due.

If the deceased had made a will, they will have appointed executors to administer their will. If no will exists and the deceased is said to have died intestate, the Court will appoint administrators. In order to administer the will, the executors or administrators must be recognised by the Court in a document called a Grant of Probate (for executors) or Letters of Administration (for Administrators). The Court will not issue this document until IHT has been paid.

Historically, personal representatives may well have been forced to take out a loan in order to pay the tax, as they could not access the deceased's assets until the tax was paid. Nowadays, some banks and building societies accept instructions from personal representatives to pay the IHT by electronic transfer out of the deceased's accounts. It should be noted that this facility is not universal, and so IHT loans are still used and remain relevant.

If the deceased individual has a will set up to divide the estate between an exempt beneficiary, such as a charity, and a non-exempt beneficiary, the estate is divided before the tax calculation so that the tax burden is on the non-exempt beneficiary.

6.8.1   Disclaimers and Deeds of Variation

There are two ways in which the terms of the will (or intestacy) can be varied after death that are effective for IHT purposes.

Disclaimers

Provided the property has not already been accepted, the beneficiary can, within two years of death, complete a written disclaimer. Provided there is no consideration in money or moneys worth in return for so doing, this will not be a transfer of value for IHT purposes and the property will, pass to the beneficiaries entitled under the will (or intestacy).

For example, a parent who is entitled to receive property from a deceased parents estate could disclaim this inheritance, safe in the knowledge that under the terms of the parents will the property would then pass to their children. They have therefore passed the property down a generation without incurring an additional IHT liability.

Deeds of Variation

Similarly, a deed of variation could be used to vary the terms of the will or intestacy for family or tax reasons. These are also known as 'deeds of family arrangement'.

The deed must be made within two years of death and, unlike the disclaimer, can actually divert property to any person or persons nominated by the person giving away their interest in the estate. For example, a potential inheritance from a parent could be diverted to a favourite charity of the beneficiaries choice. This would be effective for IHT purposes as if the deceased had left the money to charity in their will originally.

There are some conditions required, there must be no consideration in money or moneys worth, all beneficiaries giving away their inheritance must be over 18 and of sound mind and must sign the deed. If more IHT is payable as a result of the deed of variation, the Legal Personal Representatives must also sign the deed.

6.8.2   Powers of Attorney

Whilst a power of attorney is not a trust, the role of an attorney is similar to that of a trustee since they act on behalf of and for the benefit of another.

An attorney cannot give away the donors property unless there is specific permission granted in the deed.

There are two types of power of attorney who can make gifts in limited circumstances.

Enduring Powers of Attorney

This is where the donor gives to someone else the power to manage their financial affairs. The attorney can use the power immediately if that is what the donor desires. More typically, the donor makes it clear that the power is only to be used if they become mentally incapable of handling their own affairs in the future. A power of attorney is normally revoked if the donor becomes mentally incapable but under the Enduring Powers of Attorney Act 1985 a new type of power was permitted which continues when the donor becomes mentally incapable.

Under Section 3 of the Enduring Power of Attorney Act an attorney can make gifts or create trusts from the donors money where it is a reasonable gift of a seasonal nature or at a time of anniversary of a birth or marriage to persons related to or connected to the donor or to a charity to which the donor made, or might be expected to make, gifts.

Any other gifts are not allowed without court approval.

Lasting Powers of Attorney

The Mental Capacity Act 2005 created a new type of power of attorney called a lasting power of attorney. These replace enduring powers of attorney and cover welfare matters as well as financial decisions. Existing EPA's continue to have effect, but new enduring powers of attorney can no longer be created.

The position regarding gifts is almost identical to enduring powers of attorney therefore any IHT planning gifts would require permission from the Court of Protection.

6.8.3   Paying IHT on Lifetime Transfers

IHT on lifetime transfers is primarily charged on the donor, but it could also be paid by the donee. The tax is normally due six months after the end of the month of the transfer, except for transfers made between 5 April and 1 October, when the IHT is due on 30 April the following year.

When a donor dies within seven years of making a PET or chargeable transfer, any tax due is payable by the donee within six months after the end of the month of death.

7. TAX PLANNING

7.1 INTRODUCTION

Tax planning is clearly an important element of providing investment advice, but it has been correctly said that the 'tax tail shouldn't wag the advice dog'! Basically, tax is an important area of advice, but certainly not the only area.

With this in mind, the following sections set out some fairly simple tax planning strategies, conscious of the fact that each approach must be suitable for specific individual circumstances.

7.1.1 Income Tax

Each person is taxed individually in the UK, and the vast majority of UK residents benefit from at least the basic personal allowance. It makes sense that the full personal allowance is used, as this effectively is a tax-free band. There is scope, therefore, for couples to allocate the ownership of income-producing assets in the most tax-efficient way. Ignoring other considerations, it is not tax-efficient for a higher-rate taxpayer to earn interest from a savings account when their non-tax paying spouse is earning no income at all.

Even children under 18 have their own tax allowance. Grandparents and other relatives (although generally not parents, due to the '£100 income rule') may consider placing money in an income-producing investment in the name of the child.

Where an individual runs their own business, it is possible they may be able to employ a spouse (although the spouse will have to prove they have done some work to deserve the salary paid!). Often, when couples use this route, the salary is kept to just under the threshold for employer and employee National Insurance contributions (£110 a week in 2013–14).

Tax-free, or at least tax-efficient, can be attractive to many taxpayers. It is hard to see an argument against people using their ISA allowance each tax year, particularly the cash ISA allowance as everyone should have cash as an emergency fund to fall back on if needed. Stocks and shares ISAs do bear some tax in the form of the non-reclaimable 10% tax credit given to reflect the corporation tax already paid on the profits of the company, but the other advantages, such as tax-free income and capital gains, can outweigh this. Obviously, from a risk perspective, stocks and shares ISAs are not suitable for everyone.

NS&I certificates, either fixed or index-linked, provide tax-free returns and so are particularly attractive for higher-rate taxpayers. However, they are non-income-producing and so might not be suitable. Although there are no current issues available, existing index-linked issues can still roll over at the end of their term.

Other investments may be regarded as 'non income-producing' as far as the income tax system is concerned, but can provide regular returns for investors. An example of this is the 5% allowance from life assurance bonds. These are not tax-free, rather they are tax-deferred until a chargeable event occurs but, with clever planning, this chargeable event can be delayed to a time when the investor is a basic-rate taxpayer and therefore has no further liability. This form of income can also be used by someone over 65, as it will not be treated as income that could decrease their additional age allowance (provided the cumulative withdrawals do not average over 5% per annum).

At the other end of the age scale, Child Trust Funds provided tax-efficient investments for children born after 31 August 2002 and before 3 January 2011. They even benefit from an exemption from the rule under which a parent is taxable on a child's investment income of more than £100, if the capital came from the parent. For those not eligible for a CTF, Junior ISAs are available either as cash or stocks and shares.

Many individuals swear by the tax-efficient nature of pension contributions, as they are the only current UK investments that provide tax relief on contributions at an individual's highest marginal rate. The amount that can be contributed is subject to an annual limit and there is also a lifetime limit. After age 55, the investor can take 25% of the fund tax-free, but the remainder will be subject to income tax when income is taken and a special tax at death (55%). Even so, for the majority of investors, pensions contributions are tax-efficient if they are willing to suffer access restrictions. They are particularly efficient if the investor is subject to higher- and additional-rate tax while contributing, but basic rate in retirement.

Other tax-efficient investments, at the riskier end of the scale, are Enterprise Investment Schemes and Venture Capital Trusts. Both offer tax relief on contributions, provided as tax reducers (30% for EIS and for VCT contributions). However, these are highly risky investments and the tax savings may not be worth the large possibility of the investment failing completely!

7.1.2   Capital Gains Tax (CGT)

Very few private individuals actually pay any CGT, and that is not just because of the credit crunch! This is because the annual exemption, currently, £10,900, is usually enough to absorb gains, particularly if this limit is taken into account when disposing of assets. A few strategies to mitigate a CGT liability follow:

1. As with income tax, it makes sense to spread the ownership of non-exempt assets between family members to make use of the maximum number of annual exemptions.
2. For investments that can be easily segmented, it is possible to phase encashments over a number of tax years to use more than one annual allowance. Even just encashing one segment in March of a tax year, and leaving the next encashment until after 6 April, will mean that two annual allowances have been utilised.
3. Many, possibly more sophisticated, investors deliberately realise paper losses so that they can be set against future gains. As covered in the CGT chapter, this may happen without even having to sell shares if they are on HMRC's 'negligible value' list.
4. Although the act of 'bed and breakfasting' has largely been removed due to the share identification rules, it is still possible for investors to realise gains within the annual exemption and then repurchase a similar (not identical) investment. This has the other advantage of increasing the base cost of the investment. Alternatively, they can repurchase an identical investment within a tax shelter such as an ISA or pension fund.
5. The timing of a CGT payment can also be taken into account. As we saw in the CGT chapter, CGT is due on 31 January after the tax year when the gain was made. A disposal on 5 April 2013 would therefore lead to the CGT being due on 31 January 2014. Delaying the disposal by just one day, to 6 April 2013, would have delayed the due date of CGT by one full year, until 31 January 2015.
6. It is also important not to forget the CGT deferral opportunities offered by reliefs such as holdover relief, business rollover relief and reinvestment relief into EIS shares.

7.1.3   Inheritance Tax

Since the change made to the IHT rules in October 2007, allowing any unused NRB to be carried forward by a spouse/civil partner, the large market in trusts that generated a similar benefit, has diminished. There is still a market for these type of 'will trusts' for unmarried/unregistered individuals.

Most IHT planning focuses on reducing the value of an individual's estate through the use of lifetime gifts. Some of these gifts could be exempt, such as falling under the annual allowance limit, the small gifts limit or the gift limits on marriage. Even gifts that aren't exempt may well become exempt when the donor survives seven years, so it is important to start the process early and when in good health.

Gifts can also be made on a regular basis and will be exempt if they come under the 'normal expenditure' rules. This can provide a good way to reduce an estate.

Because not everyone is in the position to gift property away (or, even if they are in the position, they may not have the desire to do so), IHT planning often revolves around finding a way to pay a potential IHT bill. The most common route is that of a joint life second death whole of life policy. It is crucial that this type of plan is written under trust to avoid the policy's benefit falling into the deceased's estate and actually making the IHT situation even worse!

For donees who have received a PET that falls above the NRB, a special decreasing term assurance plan known as a 'gift *inter vivos*' policy, can cover their potential liability.

For the potential recipients of an estate that is in danger of falling above the NRB due to a previously gifted PET, a seven-year level term assurance plan can be used to cover their potential liability. After seven years, the PET will fall out of the cumulation calculation and therefore the IHT liability on the estate should fall.

These are some of the more basic approaches taken to IHT planning – it can become a very complicated world with providers trying to utilise identified loopholes which, invariably, HMRC then endeavour to remove. As with many elements of financial services, it is a constantly changing area and will undoubtedly remain so in the future.

FINANCIAL MARKETS

An exam specification breakdown is provided at the back of this workbook

1.   INTRODUCTION

In this module we will be examining the relevance of market-related factors that can influence investment decisions, processes and advice.

Some of the terminology and concepts will already be familiar to you. We will build upon this knowledge and introduce different concepts with which you may be less familiar. We hope that this will give you confidence for your examination.

You must continue reading and extending your understanding around the topics covered through additional study. This workbook does not represent everything you may be expected to know for the examination.

You will see icons or symbols alongside the text. These indicate activities or questions that have been designed to check your understanding and help you validate your understanding.

Here is a guide as to what each of the symbols means:

 Question

This identifies a question that will enable you to check your knowledge and understanding.

 Analyse

This gives you an opportunity to consider a question posed and compare your answers to the feedback given.

 Test

At the end of the module, you will have the opportunity to validate your learning by attempting questions which require knowledge of these topics.

1.1 OBJECTIVES

World Financial Markets

1. Understand the relative size of world equity markets and predominant asset sectors within each market.
2. Know the key features of the global government and corporate bond markets.
3. Understand the relative benefits, risk and costs of investing in developed and emerging markets.
4. Understand and differentiate between exchange-traded, over the counter and alternative markets.
5. Apply the principles of asset and liability matching when managing investments in different currencies.
6. Understand how indices are constructed, and the purposes and limitations of using them.

UK Markets

7. Understand the main organisations and processes for transacting, clearing, settling and safekeeping domestic financial securities.
8. Know the methods by which domestic securities are issued and brought to market.
9. Be aware of the purposes and requirements for issuing contract notes.
10. Understand the application of VAT, Stamp Duty and Stamp Duty Reserve Tax to transactions in financial services.
11. Be aware of the purposes and operation of nominee companies.

2. WORLD FINANCIAL MARKETS

2.1 SIZE OF THE WORLD MARKET

The size of the world stock market is difficult to pin down exactly. Determined by market capitalisation, it changes constantly as shares are traded on the various exchanges around the globe. At the end of 2012, the world stock market was worth in excess of $54 trillion.

By comparison, the total world derivatives market was estimated at about $791 billion, 11 times the size of the entire world economy. However, this is not a fair comparison since the derivative market is calculated using face or nominal values, many of which cancel each other out, as opposed to the real values used for valuing the stock market.

As you would imagine, there are a large number of stock markets around the world, some very large like the New York Stock Exchange (NYSE), others much smaller like the Malta Stock Exchange, where only 13 shares are listed.

We shall now look at the main exchanges around the world in turn, and examine their comparative sizes and predominant sectors.

2.2 UNITED STATES OF AMERICA

We start our world tour here, since the United States not only boasts the world's largest stock exchange (NYSE), but is also the home of another stock exchange that is larger than our own (NASDAQ).

2.2.1 New York Stock Exchange (NYSE)

Name of stock exchange	Market Value (May 2009) $m	Total annual share turnover (May 2009) $m	Market Value (Oct 2010) $m
New York Stock Exchange	9,574,066	7,986,835	12,826,262

The origin of the NYSE can be traced to 17 May 1792, when the Buttonwood Agreement was signed by 24 stockbrokers outside of 68 Wall Street, New York under a buttonwood tree.

The NYSE is now operated by NYSE Euronext, which was formed by the NYSE's 2007 merger with the fully-electronic pan European stock exchange based in Paris, Euronext.

The NYSE is one of the few exchanges which still conduct trading on the floor of the stock exchange, although most orders are now sent through to the floor electronically using a system known as superDOT.

On the trading floor, the NYSE trades in a continuous auction format, where floor traders operating out of one of the 1,500 booths, can execute stock transactions on behalf of investors. To execute their transactions, they will gather around one of the exchange's 17 trading posts where a specialist broker in that stock, who is employed by an NYSE member firm, acts as an auctioneer in an open outcry auction. The specialists do, on occasions (in fact approximately 10% of the time), facilitate the trades by committing their own capital. This can maintain an orderly market when there is a shortage of buyers and sellers. However, unlike London Stock Exchange (LSE) market makers, they are not obliged to make a market in the shares regardless of market condition. Once a trade has been made, the details are reported on the 'tape' and sent back to the broker who notifies the client who placed the order.

The NYSE is the largest stock market in terms of market capitalisation, and trades the shares of nearly 3,000 companies. As you can imagine, all stock market sectors are represented on the NYSE, although since companies in the US can only list on one domestic stock exchange, most technology companies choose to list on NASDAQ.

2.2.2 National Association of Securities Dealers Automated Quotations System (NASDAQ)

Name of stock exchange	Market Value (May 2009) $m	Total annual share turnover (May 2009) $m	Market Value (Oct 2010) $m
NASDAQ	2,773,684	12,256,704	3,653,047

Unlike the NYSE, NASDAQ is a non-centralised screen based quote driven market. There is no physical dealing floor since all business is transacted by market makers who display two way pricing on some 3,800 companies via computers linked to a worldwide network some half a million strong. It is larger than the NYSE in terms of number of companies traded and daily turnover, as the stats above confirm.

The NASDAQ is typically known as a high-tech market, attracting many of the firms dealing with the Internet or electronics. Accordingly, the stocks on this exchange are considered to be more volatile and growth-oriented. On the other hand, the companies on NYSE are perceived to be better established.

Whether a stock trades on the NASDAQ or the NYSE is not necessarily a critical factor for investors when they are making investment decisions. However, because both exchanges are perceived differently, the decision to list on a particular exchange is an important one for many companies. A company's decision to list on a particular exchange is affected also by the listing costs and requirements set by each individual exchange. The maximum listing fee on the NYSE is $250,000 while on the NASDAQ, the maximum is $150,000. The maximum continual yearly listing fees are also a big factor - they are $500,000 and $60,000 respectively.

2.3 JAPAN

2.3.1 Tokyo Stock Exchange (TSE)

Name of stock exchange	Market Value (May 2009) $m	Total annual share turnover (May 2009) $m	Market Value (Oct 2010) $m
Tokyo Stock Exchange	3,102,492	1,561,888	3,469,039

The Tokyo stock exchange is the second largest in the world, by market capitalisation.

The exchange was established on 15 May 1878, and issued government bonds to former Samurai. By the 1920s, when Japan experienced rampant growth in their economy, trading stocks over bonds, gold, and silver currencies became the norm. The exchange was shut down in 1945 and reopened in 1949 under the guidance of American authorities. Today, the TSE currently lists 2,375 domestic companies and 27 foreign companies. The TSE accounts for 90.6% of all securities transactions in Japan, dwarfing its rivals, The Osaka Stock Exchange (4.2%) and The Nagoya Stock Exchange (0.1%).

Stocks are listed on the TSE are separated into one of three 'sections':

- the First Section (for large companies) comprising about 70% of companies.
- the Second Section (for mid-sized companies) comprising about 20% of companies.
- the 'Mothers' section (for high-growth start-up companies) comprising less than 10% of companies.

As you can imagine, banks, electricals and motor manufacturers are the dominating sectors.

2.4   CHINA

China has three exchanges, the Shanghai Stock Exchange (SSE), the Hong Kong Stock Exchange and the Shenzhen Stock Exchange. All of the exchanges are governed by the China Securities Regulatory Commission (CSRC). The Shenzhen Stock Exchange is the smallest of these three, about a quarter of the size of the Shanghai Stock Exchange by market capitalisation.

Therefore we will concentrate on the first two only:

Name of stock exchange	Market Value (May 2009) $m	Total annual share turnover (May 2009) $m	Market Value (Oct 2010) $m
Shanghai Stock Exchange	2,069,937	1,685,862	2,803,493

The Shanghai Stock Exchange (SSE) was founded on 26 November 1990.

The exchange lists two different types of stocks: A and B shares. The difference between the two stocks is the currency that they are traded in. The A shares are traded in the local Renminbi yuan currency, whereas the B shares are traded in US dollars. Traditionally, A shares were not available to foreign investors. In 2003, the Chinese authorities allowed selected foreign institutions to buy A shares, having already opened the B share market to Chinese investors. The majority of the stocks listed on the exchange are A shares. There are 824 A shares and 54 B shares listed on the market.

Name of stock exchange	Market Value (May 2009) $m	Total annual share turnover (May 2009) $m	Market Value (Oct 2010) $m
Hong Kong Stock Exchange	1,773,002	519,465	4,679,387

There are over 4000 stocks listed on the Hong Kong Stock Exchange. The index for the Hong Kong exchange is called the Hang Seng, and it was introduced in 1969. The Hang Seng index consists of the 33 largest companies traded on the exchange and represents around 70% of the value of all stocks traded. As you may expect, financials and telecoms companies dominate in terms of market capitalisation.

2.5   EUROPE

2.5.1   NYSE Euronext

Name of stock exchange	Market Value (May 2009) $m	Total annual share turnover (May 2009) $m	Market Value (Oct 2010) $m
NYSE Euronext	2,262,751	742,885	2,988,977

As mentioned earlier, the NYSE Euronext is based in Paris although it has subsidiaries in Belgium, Holland, Portugal and the UK. It consists of six cash equities exchanges and six derivatives exchanges, all traded using an electronic order-driven trading system.

Euronext was formed on 22 September 2000 following a merger of the Amsterdam Stock Exchange, Brussels Stock Exchange, and Paris Bourse, in order to take advantage of the harmonisation of the European Union financial markets.

In December 2001, Euronext acquired the shares of the London International Financial Futures and Options Exchange (LIFFE), which continues to operate under its own governance.

In 2002 the group merged with the Portuguese Stock Exchange Bolsa de Valores de Lisboa e Porto (BVLP), renamed Euronext Lisbon.

The Euronext List encompasses all quoted companies. It has two segments; NextEconomy, consisting of companies whose equities are traded continuously and are active in sectors such as information technology and biotechnology, and NextPrime, consisting of companies in more traditional sectors, that are traded continuously. Inclusion in the segments is voluntary.

2.5.2   Frankfurt Stock Exchange (Deutsche Börse)

Name of stock exchange	Market Value (May 2009) $m	Total annual share turnover (May 2009) $m	Market Value (Oct 2010) $m
Frankfurt Stock Exchange	1,132,126	1,101,064	1,392,727

The Frankfurt Stock Exchange has over 90% of turnover in the German market. Trading takes place on exchange floors throughout Germany, and on an electronic order-driven platform called Xetra.

There are 6,823 companies listed on the Frankfurt Stock Exchange, and they are divided into one of three different segments, the Official Market, the Regulated Market and the Regulated Unofficial Market. This reflects the three different transparency levels on being admitted to the market, Prime, General and Entry. Companies going public by Prime and General Standards are regulated by EU rules, whereas companies choosing the Entry Standard, which is one of the easiest ways to enter the capital market, are supervised by the stock exchange itself.

Besides these market segments, there are two smaller market segments for foreign shares, from stock exchanges outside of Germany. International blue chips from Europe and the US can be traded in a special quality segment, Xetra Stars. Newex is the trading segment for central and eastern European securities on the Regulated Unofficial Market of the Frankfurt Stock Exchange.

2.5.3 London Stock Exchange (LSE)

The London Stock Exchange is the most important exchange in Europe, and one of the largest in the world. It lists over 3,000 companies and with 350 of the companies coming from 50 different countries, this makes the LSE the most international of all the exchanges.

For comparative purposes here are the figures for the London Stock Exchange.

Name of stock exchange	Market Value (May 2009) $m	Total annual share turnover (May 2009) $m	Market Value (Oct 2010) $m
London Stock Exchange	2,204,320	1,483,263	3,597,617

2.6 CONSOLIDATED LIST OF MAJOR WORLDWIDE STOCK MARKETS

For completeness, here is a consolidated list of the eight largest stock markets, by market capitalisation.

Name of stock exchange	Market Value (May 2009) $m	Total annual share turnover (May 2009) $m
New York Stock Exchange	9,574,066	7,986,835
Tokyo Stock Exchange	3,102,492	1,561,888
NASDAQ	2,773,684	12,256,704
NYSE Euronext	2,262,751	742,885
London Stock Exchange	2,204,320	1,483,263
Shanghai Stock Exchange	2,069,937	1,685,862
Hong Kong Stock Exchange	1,773,002	519,465
Frankfurt Stock Exchange	1,132,126	1,101,064

2.7 DIFFERENT MARKETS

2.7.1 Exchange-Traded Market

A stock exchange, such as those we have covered in this section, provides trading facilities for stockbrokers and traders. To be able to trade a security on a particular stock exchange, it has to be listed there.

There is usually no compulsion to issue stock via the stock exchange itself, and such trading is said to be 'off-exchange' or 'over-the-counter' (OTC).

2.7.2   Over-The-Counter (OTC)

OTC trading is the name given to the trade of financial instruments directly between two parties, bypassing the 'middle-man' of an exchange. The process is used predominantly for derivatives and bond trading, although it can be used for other securities. This gives greater flexibility to use bespoke, non-standard and complex products, however, it is less visible, regulated and measurable than a transaction undertaken via an exchange. The complexity of some such products has led to very big losses in some cases by very large companies, which did not fully understand the product they were buying.

If a company's stock is traded OTC, it may be because the company is small and unable to meet the listing requirements of exchanges. These types of securities are traded by broker-dealers negotiating directly with each other via computers or over the phone.

2.7.3   Alternative Markets

ICAP Securities and Derivatives Exchange Limited

In May 2012 PLUS Markets plc announced that, following the termination of the formal sale process announced to the market on 3 February 2012, the company intended to commence a process of orderly closure of the regulated activities undertaken by it, including the operation of PLUS's cash equities recognised investment exchange. ICAP purchased the securities business from PLUS Markets.

BATS Trading Ltd

BATS is a pan-European MTF for equities operating under the brand name of BATS Chi-X Europe. BATS Chi-X Europe was formed through the combination of two MTFs in 2011 (BATS Europe and Chi-X Europe) and is a wholly owned subsidiary of BATS Global Markets Inc., an operator of stock and options markets in the US and Europe. BATS Chi-X Europe supports competition and drives innovation in the European equities markets. It offers trading in more than 1,800 of the most liquid equities across

Multilateral Trading Facilities

Since the implementation of MiFID, entities trading in financial instruments have been able to set up in one of two forms – as an exchange or as a multilateral trading facility (MTF).

Different standards and rules apply to each, with MTFs being less restricted. The instruments traded on MTFs are not subject to the same strict regulation as those traded on standard markets.

MTFs are not formal, physical exchanges but alternative trading venues that bring together multiple third party buyers and sellers of securities, which participants access remotely. They often route orders through 'dark pools', which are non-displayed, matching engines for large orders. Their aim is to increase matching rates and give better execution.

Since their launch, they have taken significant trading business away from the more established exchanges, and some commentators predict that they will account for '20% of European equity orders by the end of 2009' and 'half of the European share trading (market) within the next four to five years'.

Their business models are based on providing efficient service and charging very low fees, to attract high volumes of business. The share prices of the more formal existing venues have decreased, and they have been forced into investing in new technology, to be able to compete.

The Fidessa Fragmentation Index available at http://fragmentation.fidessa.com, provides weekly figures detailing European trading venues, and splits out for each venue, the per cent share of trades in equities, per index.

To give you an indication of the market share that the MTF's have taken, as at August 2009, the market share for FTSE 100 equity trades was divided as follows:

Venue	Share
LSE	65.05%
Chi-x	20.72%
Turquoise	8.96%
BATS	4.02%
NASDAQ OMX	1.25%

The MTF's providing alternative trading venues for FTSE 100 equities are:

Chi-X

This is a pan-European exchange providing an order driven platform for trading equities, operated by Instinet. It was launched in March 2007.

It provides an alternative venue for trading equities listed on the LSE, Frankfurt Stock Exchange, Euronext and OMX.

It offers both a visible order book and introduced an invisible book (dark pool) called Chi-Delta in April 2009.

Trades are cleared through EMCF (European Multilaterial Clearing Facility).

Further information can be found at www.chi-x.com.

Turquoise

This is also an equities trading platform, launched in September 2008 and created by a group of nine major investment banks. It was set up to rival European exchanges.

It currently trades in excess of 1,600 stocks across 15 markets and according to the FFI in August 2009, it has picked up 6.06% of the Europe-wide market.

It provides both dark and visible orders.

Trading Platform – Cinnober.

Clearing and settlement – Clearing – European Central Counterparty 'ECC'. Settlement – Citigroup's Global Transaction Services.

Further information can be found at www.tradeturquoise.com.

BATS Europe

Launched October 2008, it is another pan-European MTF. In addition to its market share for FTSE 100 equity trades, in August 2009 it accounted for 3.98% of the French CAC 40, 3.85% of the German Dax, 2.86% of the Belgian BEL 20 index and 3.28% of the Dutch AEX index, equity trades.

Clearing & settlement – European Multilateral Clearing Facility 'EMCF' (Fortis product).

Further information can be found at www.batstrading.co.uk.

NASDAQ OMX Europe

A smaller pan-European MTF, which was launched in September 2008. It operates visible orders and from August 2009 will also start routing orders to non-displayed liquidity venues, including NEURO Dark, its own dark platform.

Clearing & settlement – 'EMCF'.

Further information can be found at www.nasdaqomxeurope.com.

Future Developments

There is significant competition in the sector and a fragmented marketplace. There have been criticisms that transparency in the market has reduced since the introduction of a range of transaction reporting facilities.

3.   EMERGING MARKETS

3.1   INTRODUCTION

The term emerging markets can be defined in different ways:

- Markets in those counties described by the World Bank as low or middle income; and
- Markets with a stock capitalisation of less than 2% of the total world market.

3.2   BENEFITS OF INVESTING IN EMERGING MARKETS

- **Faster economic growth** – developing nations tend to grow at a faster rate than those countries that are well developed, as they try to catch up in terms of living standards and, in the process, develop their infrastructure and financial systems.
- **Savings rates** are usually higher in underdeveloped countries. Foreign direct investment will have a positive benefit on the economy, leading to rapid economic growth. This will lead to a rapid growth in profits.
- **Inefficient pricing** – it is possible to exploit pricing anomalies in underdeveloped economies, where analysis and research on companies are not so well advanced.
- **Industry representation** – there may be the opportunity for investors to gain exposure to different types of industry, not possible in other well developed countries.

- **Attractive valuations** – historically, emerging markets have traded at a discount to developed nations.
- **Low correlation of returns** – historically, there has been a low correlation between the fortunes of developed and emerging markets. This provides the investor with an opportunity for diversification.

3.3 DRAWBACKS OF INVESTING IN EMERGING MARKETS

- **Restrictions on foreign ownership** – some underdeveloped counties impose restrictions on foreigners owning shares in certain companies.
- **Foreign exchange restrictions** – due to restrictions imposed by the emerging nation, it may not be possible to repatriate funds to the UK, once the investor has disinvested.
- **Taxation** – whilst double taxation agreements are in place with most if not all developed nations, there may be local taxes imposed by developing nations that are not covered by existing treaties, thereby adding to the tax burden.
- Additional costs may be incurred, for example commission on foreign currency, costs of transferring the money, nominee costs and possibly translation or legal costs.
- **Lack of transparency** – there is likely to be a lower quality and transparency of information from emerging markets, compared to countries that are well developed.

3.4 RISKS OF INVESTING IN EMERGING MARKETS

- **Political** – emerging markets tend to be less politically stable. This could have a devastating effect on foreign investment. For example, new laws could be passed which outlaw the holding of certain investments by foreign persons, inhibit the ability to repatriate funds or impose high levels of taxation.
- **Volatility** – emerging markets are more volatile than developed ones and are prone to banking or other crises. Lack of information can result in a 'herding' of foreign investment into a small number of companies, which will see a sharp rise, but could be followed by an equally sharp fall, if foreign investment is withdrawn from one of these companies in the future.
- **Liquidity** – emerging markets are more concentrated ie, less liquid than developed markets. Investments are generally less marketable and therefore tend to trade with much wider spreads.
- **Capital** – custody and settlement may be far more difficult to arrange, and the potential for fraud may be increased with less developed regulatory protection and problems with translation. Understanding a contract in English can be difficult enough without the added complication of interpreting complex terms in a foreign language.
- **Currency risk** – emerging markets tend to have weaker currencies, which are far more susceptible to sudden movements following the withdrawal of foreign investment. Any loss incurred on the exchange rate will reduce, and could exceed, the potential gains on the investment capital.

EXAMPLE

John invests £50,000 in an emerging market, Westonia. The investments have done well for him but the political climate is changing, an election is due and the people in the know, think that the opposition will seek to restrict the withdrawal of foreign investment, should they get to power. John decides to encash his investments, which are falling in value due to the political uncertainties, and 'escapes' with a gain of 10% on his initial investment. However, he now has to repatriate the funds and he is staggered to discover that the pound is now 30% stronger against the local currency than it was when he invested his capital in Westonia. He makes an overall loss of 20%.

Asset and Liability Management

The definition of asset and liability management, is a risk management technique to earn an adequate return, whilst maintaining a comfortable surplus of assets beyond liabilities. This now takes into consideration a number of variable factors such as interest rates, currency exchange rates, earning power and a degree of willingness to take on debt. This is also called surplus management.

The early origins of asset and liability management date to the high interest rate periods in the mid to late 1970s and early 1980s in the United States. Previously, a bank could, for example, borrow money for a year at 5% and lend the same money at 5.5% to a highly rated borrower for five years. This appears to be a good transaction for the bank, but with it came risk; when the bank came to refinance their loan, interest rates may have risen and they may have had to pay a higher rate on the new financing, than the fixed 5.5% they are earning on the loan. There was a potential mismatch between assets and liabilities, a mismatch that could be shown in the market value (immediate) method of accounting, but not so immediately in the accruals method of accounting.

This was not such a problem before the 1970s, as interest rates in developed countries were relatively stable, so losses due to asset-liability mismatches were negligible. With yield curves generally upward sloping (a 'normal' yield curve), banks could exploit the market by borrowing short and lending long.

In the 1970s, and into the early 1980s, a period of volatile interest rates ensued. Many firms, who had been used to operating on the accruals accounting basis, did not recognise the risks they were taking until it was too late, and the loss itself had been accrued. Many large firms went to the wall.

In response to this, managers of financial firms focussed on asset-liability risk. The focus was not so much on whether the value of assets might fall, or that the value of liabilities might rise, it was more on the fact that capital might be depleted by a narrowing of the difference between assets and liabilities. In essence, we are talking about a cash-flow risk here, as the capital of most financial institutions is small relative to their assets or liabilities, so a small change in assets or liabilities can be translated into large percentage changes in capital. We only have to look at the situation over the last couple of years, and the 'credit crunch', to see this in practice.

A number of different techniques were used to analyse the risks, and became known as asset-liability management (ALM). These included such techniques as 'gap analysis' and 'duration analysis', which worked well if both assets and liabilities comprised fixed cash flows.

A more expansive technique is that of 'scenario analysis' where several interest rate are specified for the following five or ten years. Many different scenarios would be examined, anticipating very different behaviours throughout the entire yield curve. Assumptions would then be made as to how assets and liabilities would perform under each scenario. Based upon these assumptions, the performance of a firm's balance sheet could be projected for each scenario. If the projected performance was particularly poor under certain scenarios, the firm could adjust assets or liabilities (or both) to address the situation.

ALM has evolved greatly since the 1980s. The growth of the derivatives market has helped facilitate a variety of hedging techniques (for example, a utility company's hedging of gas prices can be presented as a form of ALM). There has also been a major development in the securitisation market, allowing firms to directly address asset-liability risk by removing assets or liabilities from their balance sheet. Again, we have witnessed the fall-out from this securitisation development during the credit crunch.

The scope of ALM has also increased, which is why we are including it in this section. Along with interest-rate exposures and liquidity risk, ALM techniques are being adopted to address foreign exchange risk so that the situation described above of John's investment in Westonia can be avoided by corporations.

4. THE UK MARKETS

4.1 INTRODUCTION

The London Stock Exchange (LSE) is a recognised investment exchange (RIE) and, as such, is answerable to the FCA. The LSE has a responsibility to *'ensure that the operation of each of its markets is orderly and provides proper protection to investors, and to promote and maintain high standards of integrity and fair dealing'*.

Its main responsibilities include:

*   Providing a primary and secondary market for equities and fixed interest securities;
*   Supervising member firms;
*   Regulating the market;
*   Recording all deals;
*   Disseminating price sensitive information received via its Regulatory News Service (RNS).

4.2 MEMBER FIRMS OF THE LSE

All member firms are broker dealers. As such, they can act in one of two capacities:

*   Act as agent on behalf of the customer where they take a commission (broker).
    *   Here they will receive an order from a non-member client and will arrange the trade with another member firm for a commission.
    *   Alternatively they may have an order to purchase, and a matching order to sell, from another client. They can act as agent to an agency cross-transaction, charging a commission to both parties but offering the same price to both parties.
*   Act as principal where they trade their own book (dealers).
    *   They will be selling shares held on the firm's own books to the client.

Market makers provide liquidity to the market by making a two-way price (bid offer spread), using a screen-based system to display their prices. Broker dealers can see the prices being offered and place their orders based on the quoted prices.

Most of the equity dealing is conducted via a range of electronic systems hosted by the LSE, as follows:

4.3 SETS

The Stock Exchange Electronic Trading Service (SETS) is an electronic order driven service trading FTSE 100, FTSE 250 and the FTSE Small Cap Index constituents, as well as other securities.

Additional functionality following changes in the rules under MiFID, means that SETS now also provides market maker support for all stocks deemed to be 'liquid' under MiFID definitions.

It allows buyers and sellers to be matched, thus avoiding the need to go through a market maker who would charge a spread.

Order Book

The following types of order are permissible:

- **At best** – this specifies the number of shares to be bought or sold, and is executed immediately at the best possible price. The main problem that can occur is if the market for the stock is very thin (illiquid), the spread may widen considerably, particularly at either end of the trading day. The bargain is, however, being executed whatever the price and may therefore secure a very poor price for the client.
- **Limit** – these are the only orders which remain on the screen. The client will specify the number of shares required to be bought or sold and the maximum (purchase) or minimum (sale) price they are prepared to accept.
- **Execute and eliminate** – these orders have a quantity and limit price. If it cannot be filled in its entirety, then the deal can be partially filled but the remaining part of the deal is abandoned.
- **Fill or kill** – these orders may be limited to a particular price, and if not filled in full, then the entire deal is abandoned. It is possible to leave the price open, in which case the order will rely on the depth of the order book.
- **Market** – this is an 'at best' order which is held on the order book during an auction call period. These deals are given top priority for matching at the end of the auction period, according to the time they were submitted.
- **Iceberg** – these orders allow market participants to enter large orders onto the order book with only a certain specified portion of the order visible to the market. The order must have details of the total size of the order and the specified amount to be made visible. Once the peak is entirely dealt with, the system automatically keeps reintroducing orders until the entire amount is dealt.
- **New order types** – 2009:
  - **Hidden limit orders** – these are limit orders where both the price and volume are hidden. Unlike Iceberg orders where the peak is continually 'refreshed' and displayed, participants will have no idea if there is any remaining order or not. They are only available for large orders meeting certain threshold conditions.
  - **Hidden pegged orders** – these orders allow participants to peg their order to the best bid, offer or mid price.

An example of an order book follows:

BUY			SELL		
Price	**Time**	**Volume**	**Price**	**Time**	**Volume**
360	11.10	4,000	361	11.18	3,000
360	11.15	2,000	361	11.24	2,000
359	11.06	1,000	362	11.04	5,000
359	11.08	2,000	362	11.09	3,000

 What would the order book look like if a limit order to sell 8,000 at no worse than 360p was submitted at 11.25?

The answer follows:

BUY			SELL		
Price	**Time**	**Volume**	**Price**	**Time**	**Volume**
359	11.06	1,000	360	11.25	2,000
359	11.08	2,000	361	11.18	3,000
			361	11.24	2,000
			362	11.04	5,000
			362	11.09	3,000

The order would have been partially filled with 6,000 shares being sold at 360, leaving 2,000 shares on the order book.

The order book can be seen by any market participants, and a yellow strip on the SETS screen will display the best prevailing buy and sell prices for each security. Orders that are put through the order book must be executed at best price. Both member firms are given notification of the trade once it is settled, and the deal is automatically reported to the LSE.

Only LSE firms and SETS participants (members of EU exchanges authorised to conduct SETS trades) can input orders.

A Central Counterparty (CCP) service exists for all deals executed on SETS, which enables trades to be conducted anonymously and guarantees trades removing counterparty risk. Participants can now use either LCH.Clearnet Ltd or SIX x-clear as their CCP for SETS trades.

Trades are normally settled through the CREST system, operated by Euroclear UK & Ireland.

Orders outside the order book are permitted, provided that they are satisfied by the best bid or offer price on the order book. If they cannot be settled at that price, they must be settled at the volume weighted average price or better.

All deals on SETS are settled on a **T+3** basis, ie, three business days after the date of trade.

4.4   SEAQ

Unlike SETS, SEAQ is a **quote-driven** screen based system for trading.

This means that member firms can act as market makers, and compete with each other by making two prices in stocks, in the hope of attracting business from other members (known as broker dealers). Since all market makers must quote real-time two-way prices in all market conditions and act as willing counterparties to trades, they are often required to commit their own capital when there is a lack of market liquidity.

SEAQ is for the following securities:

*   fixed interest market, and
*   AIM securities not traded on SETS or SETSqx.

The quotes must appear between the mandatory period of 8.00am and 4.30pm, and apply to any deal no greater than the historic size of the average institutional trade in the shares, known as **normal market size** (NMS). This is shown on SEAQ as the minimum quote size (MQS).

Throughout the day, the best prices are shown by the yellow strip and are referred to as the **touch**. This is the price at which a broker dealer is obliged to transact, subject only to size, in order to fulfil **best execution** requirements. Deals outside the normal market size would need to be negotiated with the broker dealer. The minimum permitted price change is called the **tick size** (generally 0.1p, 0.25p, 0.5p or 1p depending on the price and liquidity of the share).

If the best bid price was equal to the best ask price, it would be called a **choice price**.

If the bid price was greater than the ask price, it is called a **back** or a **backwardation**.

The SEAQ system offers a screen which changes colour depending on the last price movement of the security, blue for an upward price movement red for a downward movement and green for an unchanged price.

Remember that SEAQ is a quotation system, not a dealing system. If a firm wants to deal, they must telephone the firm and arrange the transaction.

In order to ensure a transparent market, all trades conducted within the mandatory quote period are reported to the LSE by market makers within three minutes. This is known as **trade reporting**.

The LSE publish the size and price of trades up to six times NMS on SEAQ immediately, a process known as **publication**. Trades greater than six times NMS have delayed reporting for one hour. Very large trades (over 75 times NMS) can be withheld from the market for up to five days, to enable the market maker to unwind a large position without the market going against him. Market makers can deal anonymously through specialist firms known as Inter Dealer Brokers (IDB's), in order to facilitate this. They can also borrow stock from stock borrowing and lending intermediaries (SBLI's) to help preserve market liquidity.

4.5   SETSqx

The Stock Exchange Electronic Trading Service – quotes and crosses (SETSqx) is the trading platform used for securities that are less liquid than those on SETS.

SETSqx combines the features of the SEAQ market maker model, and supports it with some additional electronic order book functionality.

How does it work?

- Market makers must provide continuous prices throughout the trading day, and have obligations which are similar to those on SEAQ. The mandatory quote period is slightly different and they have the option to participate in the electronic auctions.
- In addition to trades being executed through market makers, there are four auctions 'uncrossings' that take place daily at 8.00am, 11.00am, 3.00pm, and 4.35pm. During these auctions, the system works like the order book, and matches as many orders as possible.

At other times during the day, the system continues to work as a quote-driven system.

Because of the limited liquidity in the securities traded on SETSqx, Iceberg and Market order are not supported, although different types of limit order are.

4.6   TRADING IN GILTS

Gilts are traded in a similar way to the quote-driven trading of equities. Broker dealers are permitted to deal both as principal and agent, very much like their equity counterparts. For example, the rules for trade reporting of gilt deals are the same as for equity deals.

The main difference is in the way gilt market makers operate. Gilt-edged market makers (GEMMs) undertake to the Debt Management Office (DMO) to make two-way prices in a range of securities in any conditions, not to the stock exchange.

GEMMS report daily to the FCA in terms of their financial stability, and are not under an obligation to display daily prices on SEAQ (in fact this system is used very little for gilts).

As SEAQ is rarely used in the gilt market, a broker will need to phone around to establish the best price for the size of deal. A firm that is not a GEMM will need to take all reasonable steps to make sure that the transaction price is better than the best price available from a registered market maker.

GEMMS have a choice as to whether to deal in non index-linked gilts only, index-linked gilts only, or both.

Inter dealer brokers (IDBs) are set up as separate companies, although they can be subsidiaries of broker/dealers. Their role is to act as a matching agent for market makers who wish to undo their positions with them, and maintain confidentiality. They do this by settling as principal, thereby maintaining the anonymity of the market makers involved. Keeping this secretive theme, prices displayed on IDB computer screens are not available to brokers or clients, just to market makers. It should be noted that IDBs also operate in equity quote-driven markets, such as SEAQ, which we have described earlier.

The normal settlement timing for trades in gilts is **T+1**, ie, 1 business day after the trade date.

The electronic Order book for Retail Bonds (ORB) was established by the LSE on 1 February 2010 to provide a more liquid and transparent market in retail bonds.

EU regulations distinguish between 'wholesale' (typically denominations of £50,000 or greater) and 'retail' (usually £1,000, some £5,000 or £10,000).

At the moment most corporate bonds are wholesale; the secondary market for retail bonds is fragmented, usually over-the-counter (OTC); therefore most private investors use corporate bond funds rather than dealing directly.

The ORB provides a similar facility that for share trading for a select number of gilts, supranational organisations, and UK corporate bonds.

Investors can enter orders on the order book either directly, if a sophisticated investor, or via a broker who offers Direct Market Access (DMA).

Dedicated market makers also provide two-way prices.

The market operates with an opening auction phase between 8.00 and 8.45am and closes at 4.30pm.

Most corporate bonds are traded in lot sizes of £1,000; the standard lot size for gilts is £1; the 'tick' size is 1p for both.

4.6.1   The Gilt Repo Market

'Repo' is short for 'sale and repurchase' agreement. One party agrees to sell gilts to another party, but with a formal agreement to buy equivalent securities from them at an agreed price and on a specific date. It is therefore a form of secured borrowing, with the gilt itself used as collateral.

The interest rate generated by the difference between the sale and repurchase prices, is the 'repo' rate.

All participants in the gilt market are free to utilise repo transactions.

A **reverse repo** occurs when gilts are purchased first, with an agreement to sell back in the future. This allows market participants to go short in the market.

Agreements to repurchase at a specific date are known as **'term repos'**. There are also **'open repos'** where there is no set redemption date, and contracts roll over on a daily basis until one of the parties decides to cancel the deal. There are also **'overnight repos'** which, unsurprisingly, applies to any repo where the settlement date is the next day.

4.6.2   Gilt Strips

'Strips' is the acronym for 'Separately Traded Registered Interest and Principal Securities', meaning certain gilts can be stripped into their individual cash flows of interest and principal payments. They are explained further in Module 5.

Only a GEMM, the DMO or the Bank of England can strip or reconstitute a strippable gilt, although, once done, anyone can trade or hold strips.

4.7   TRADING IN THE UK FIXED INTEREST MARKET

This market includes local authority bonds, listed corporate bonds and some Eurobonds, but excludes gilts. As a result, it is smaller and deemed less important than the gilts market.

The DMO is not involved in this market. Market makers are registered with the LSE, who impose the dealing obligation for market makers to buy and sell up to a marketable quantity of stock at a firm price. This 'marketable quantity' is determined by the LSE. Apart from the absence of the DMO, the overall operation of the market is very similar as that for gilts.

The rules for trade reporting are the same as for gilt and equity deals.

The normal settlement timing for trades in the UK fixed interest market is **T+3**, ie, three business days after the trade date.

4.8   AMERICAN AND GLOBAL DEPOSITARY RECEIPTS

4.8.1   American Depositary Receipts (ADRs)

An ADR is a dollar-denominated negotiable instrument issued by a depositary bank in respect of non-US listed shares that have been lodged with the bank.

These were originally designed to enable US investors to invest in overseas shares without the high dealing costs and delayed settlement associated with overseas investment. However, they are now also used by UK institutional investors wishing to purchase UK-listed shares therefore avoiding stamp duty. Stamp duty reserve tax is paid on creation of the ADR but not on subsequent dealing.

Up to 20% of a company's voting share capital may be converted into ADRs and many UK companies have used ADRs as a means of raising capital. Sometimes more than one share is deposited to make up one ADR for example 1 ADR = 10 shares.

ADRs are denominated in US dollars. Dividends are paid to the holding bank in the currency of the overseas company and paid to the holder of the ADR in dollars.

ADRs are traded on the NYSE, NASDAQ and are also traded in the UK through SEAQ.

4.8.2   Global Depositary Receipts (GDRs)

Depository receipts issued outside the US are known as Global Depositary Receipts. Again, shares are deposited in a bank which issues the GDR.

GDRs are often listed in the Luxembourg Stock Exchange and in the LSE, where they are traded on the International Order Book (IOB).

4.8.3   International Order Book, International Bulletin Board and International Retail Service

International Order Book

The international order book, offered by the LSE, offers easy and cost efficient access for traders looking to invest in fast growing economies, for example, in Central and Eastern Europe, Asia and the Middle East via depositary receipts (DRs).

The service is based on an order-driven electronic order book similar to SETS, but with the added option for member firms to display their identity pre-trade by using Named Orders, offering greater visibility in the market.

Deals are quoted in US dollars with trading available from 9.00am until 15.30pm.

International Bulletin Board

This no longer exists. All remaining securities that were historically traded on International Bulletin Board (TradElect segments: ITBB & ITBU) have been migrated to SETSqx as part of the December 2009 quarterly review that took effect on Wednesday 16 December 2009.

International Retail Service

The International Retail Service (IRS) is a service provided by the LSE that allows UK investors to trade in overseas stocks quoted in sterling without having to worry about exchange rates through the CREST system. This allows shares to be held in dematerialised form. Not all international equities are listed on the IRS. There are currently around 330 large cap equities available, primarily European and US companies.

	International Order Book	**International Retail Service**
Market type	Order driven	Quote driven
Securities Traded	ADRs/GDRs	US and European blue chip equities
Currency	US dollars	Sterling
Market Makers	No	Yes (committed principals – CPs)
Settlement	Bilaterally directly with counterparty; Euroclear Bank or DTCC	CREST depository interests
Trading	9.00 – 15.30 Opening/closing auctions; continuous trading in between	7.00 – 17.00 (Mandatory Quote Period for most European stocks 8.15 – 16.00)

4.9 SETTLEMENT

We will now look briefly at the clearing and settlement procedures for UK domestic financial securities.

The process of clearing and settlement involves a number of stages:

Confirmation

The details of the deal are confirmed. This involves both sides of the transaction being compared to ensure they match.

Clearing

For trades on SETS, LCH.Clearnet or SIX x-clear becomes the central counterparty to each trade. The parties calculate their liabilities and position themselves for settlement.

Settlement

The securities are transferred into the name of the new owner, against payment. This system whereby the securities are only transferred against simultaneous payment, is known as Delivery versus Payment' (DvP). The converse of this is that the buyer will not release the cash unless it is against the simultaneous transfer of the securities. From this perspective, it is described as 'Cash against Delivery' (CAD). This system of settlement provides security for both the seller and the buyer of the securities.

A system for delivery **free of payment** is also available.

Settlement Periods

The UK markets operate a rolling settlement system. For UK equities and corporate bonds, the settlement period is T+3 (trade date plus three business days) and gilts are settled T+1. Trades that settle on the next working day are described as 'cash settled'.

4.9.1 CREST

The CREST settlement system is used for UK and Irish securities markets. It settles transactions in equities, corporate bonds and commercial paper, gilts and treasury bills and money market instruments, CD's and a range of international securities, and can facilitate settlement in £, US$ or euro's.

CREST offers investors the opportunity to hold their shares in dematerialised form (where there is no certificate issued evidencing ownership, just an electronic record), either in their own name within CREST, or in the name of their nominee company. Additionally, deals can be settled through CREST, and paper certificates held outside the system.

How Does the CREST System Work?

*   **Structure**

    Members have securities in accounts in CREST (much in the same way as we have money in a bank account). There are different types of member depending upon their technical ability to interface with the system. Individuals wishing to hold stocks in CREST are known as CREST sponsored members, but can only do so through an institution which has the technical ability to interface with CREST, known as a CREST member (eg, a stockbroking firm). The individual beneficial owner will appear on the company register as the recorded legal owner of the shares that they have in their CREST accounts. Balances are 'dynamic', ie, they continually change as settlement occurs.

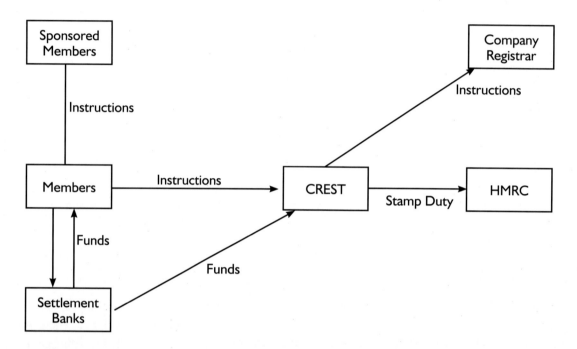

*   **Settlement Banks**

    Each member must have a contractual arrangement with their bank, guaranteeing the settlement of their CREST transactions up to an amount known as a 'debit cap' (think of it as akin to an overdraft limit).

    CREST records each member's obligations (purchases/sales) on a **Cash Memorandum Account** (CMA) on a real time basis throughout the day. At the end of the day, the net position has to be settled by the members' settlement bank with CREST. Settlement banks maintain liquidity balances with the Bank of England specifically for the settlement of CREST liabilities.

    The amount of unused facility (credit) at any point during the day, is known as the **headroom**. Using our overdraft analogy, it is the unused portion of our overdraft limit.

*   **Company Registrars**

    Company registrars are required under the Companies Acts, to maintain a list of their shareholders. As trades settle, CREST issues **Register Update Requests** (RUR's) to the company registrars, instructing them to update their shareholder register. It may take companies a little while to up-date their records, so it is worth noting that ownership legally passes at the point of payment, even if the records are not updated until later in the day.

*   **Revenue Authority**

    CREST acts as collector of transfer tax (stamp duty) for the relevant tax authorities.

The CREST Process In Order...

Trade date:

*   The trade and price is agreed through the exchange.
*   Each member (the buying and selling members) create a settlement instruction, and send it to CREST.

On or just after the trade date:

*   CREST compares both settlement instructions, ensures that the details are correct and 'match'.

Settlement date:

*   CREST sends details of the trade to SSE for settlement.
*   SSE checks that the seller has sufficient securities, that the buyer has sufficient headroom and that the buyers bank has sufficient liquidity with the Bank of England.

If so the transaction is settled:

*   The securities are simultaneously moved from the selling members account to the buying members account.
*   Funds are transferred from the buying settlement bank to the seller's settlement bank.
*   The CMA of the buyer is debited and the CMA of the seller is credited.
*   The SSE send confirmation that the trade has settled, to CREST.
*   CREST sends a RUR to the company registrar, to update the register of shareholders.

Each business day, between 5.00am and 4.30pm, CREST attempts to settle transactions. This can be done as long as the transaction has reached its settlement date and there are sufficient resources available to allow the transaction to settle.

5.   HOW UK SECURITIES ARE ISSUED

5.1   GILTS

The market in UK government bonds ('gilts') is managed by the Debt Management Office (DMO), an executive agency of the Treasury.

The DMO manages the governments Public Sector Net Cash Requirement (PSNCR), which is the difference between government revenue and government expenditure. The DMO issues new gilts each week, by auction. Gilt issues of over £200 billion are expected for 2009–10.

Auction Process

- Large investors submit competitive bids at the price and quantity of stock required.
- If successful, they pay the price **they** bid.
- Individuals can submit **non-competitive bids** for amounts up to £500,000 nominal (market makers can bid non-competitively for no more than 0.5% of the gilt on auction). If successful they are allocated the stock at the **average price** of all accepted bids.
- 'When issued', trading is allowed on the stock exchange. This occurs between the announcement of the auction, and when the gilts are actually issued, ie, at the auction itself.
- Once a gilt is issued, it can be traded in the secondary bond market.

Rarely, but occasionally, gilt auctions fail. The first failure of a gilt auction since 2002 occurred on 25 March 2009.

> **LONDON (Reuters) – Britain suffered its first failed government bond auction since 2002 on Wednesday, after bids fell more than 100 million pounds short of the 1.75 billion pounds the government was trying to raise.**
>
> **Gilt prices initially tumbled, but market strategists said the result did not suggest Britain was facing an incipient funding crisis as it prepares to issue a record amount of gilts this year and next to fund extra spending through the recession.**
>
> **Instead, they blamed opaque Bank of England gilt-buying plans for the fact the UK Debt Management Office (DMO) could not find enough bidders for the 2049 gilt at an auction, where there would usually be heavy demand from pension funds and insurers.**

Where this happens, the stock becomes a 'tap stock' and it is then released slowly when the price reaches pre-determined levels.

When the demand for a gilt is high, the DMO can issue further blocks of a particular gilt. These are known as tranches.

Syndicated Offers

With a syndicated offer, the DMO, on behalf of the government, appoints a group of banks to manage the sale of a gilt on its behalf. A Lead Manager and Co-Lead Managers are appointed, who advise and market the gilt to investors.

Potential investors are approached to find out how much of the issue they are prepared to buy, and at what price. From this information, a book of demand is constructed. The book closes, and the issue is priced when the Lead Manager agrees that the size and quality of the book meets the issuer (DMO's) objectives. The gilts are then allocated to the investors.

Syndicated offers had only been used once before 2009. This method was used for an offer in June 2009, and the DMO plans to use this process for up to a further eight issues as part of its 2009–10 financing remit, raising £25 billion through the issue of both long-dated and index-linked gilts.

5.2   HOW EQUITIES ARE ISSUED

There are, two types of company, private limited companies and public limited companies (plcs).

Only plc's can issue shares to the general public, and have their shares publicly traded on a recognised stock exchange. In practice, only a proportion of plc's choose to do so. Some choose to be listed on the London Stock Exchange's Alternative Investment Market (AIM), rather than seek a full listing.

5.2.1   Full Listing

There are strict criteria for private companies, to gain a full listing known as listing rules.

These rules are laid down by the FCA, who act as the competent authority for listing, referred to as the UK Listing Authority (UKLA). In this capacity, they also maintain the Official List detailing all the companies listed on the LSE.

These rules include the following requirements:

- Market capitalisation of at least £700,000 with at least 25% of shares freely available to the public (known as the free float).
- Market value of any bonds to be listed must be at least £200,000.
- There cannot be any restrictions on the sale of the shares (this is to avoid the situation of family companies who sometimes place a restriction on selling shares in the company).
- No one can have more than 30% of the voting rights.
- There must be three years of audited accounts available.
- The directors must have appropriate experience and expertise.
- There are slightly less stringent rules for companies in certain sectors, eg, scientific research based activities, provided they have the requisite three years trading experience.

5.2.2   Listing on AIM

Gaining admission to the Alternative Investment Market (AIM) is far less onerous, since the minimum capitalisation level, free float and trading record, are not required. As a result, most AIM companies are in their early stages of development, with the intention of seeking a full listing at a later date.

The requirements for seeking a listing on aim are as follows:

- A **nominated adviser (NOMAD)** must be appointed. Their role is to advise directors of their responsibilities under AIM rules, and the content required in the prospectus that they must issue, in order to be admitted to AIM.
- A nominated broker must also be appointed. Other than providing information about the company to interested parties, their role is primarily to make a market and facilitate trading in the shares of the company.

5.2.3   New Issues Methods

If the company wishes to raise more capital through their listing or admission, this is done via an **Initial Public Offering (IPO)**.

These are four types of IPO, which are also known as marketing operations. The fifth method of achieving a listing – known as an 'introduction' – raises no new capital.

Offer for Sale

- The company sells its shares to an issuing house. These do not necessarily have to be new shares. For example, family shareholdings could be offered to the public in this way.
- The issuing house then invites applications from the general public, based on a detailed prospectus known as an offering document. For AIM share listing, a less detailed prospectus is necessary, but there must be a warning about investing in smaller company shares. The prospectus is prepared by the directors, but assessed by an independent sponsor (usually either a solicitor or an accountant).
- The independent sponsor must also provide a letter to the UKLA, confirming working capital adequacy. This normally accompanies the prospectus.
- An advert will also be placed in a national newspaper detailing the flotation. This is known as a formal notice.
- The offer price will be slightly higher than the price paid to the company.
- The offer can be on either a fixed or tender price basis.

Fixed Price Offer

- The price is fixed just below the price at which the offer is expected to be fully subscribed, in order to ensure an active secondary market.
- Potential investors subscribe for a particular number of shares at the fixed price.
- If, as usually is the case due to the price setting criteria, the issue is over-subscribed, the shares are allocated by either a scaling down or by a random selection from the applications received, as detailed in the offer document.

Pricing the offer is a difficult task, since there is a delicate balance between encouraging an active secondary market whilst avoiding an excessive over-subscription, which may indicate that the company has not raised as much capital as it could have done. In addition, market sentiment could change between the date of the offer and the closing date for applications. For this reason, some companies may prefer to issue the shares on a tender basis.

Tender Offer

- Rather than fixing a price, invitations for tenders are sought from prospective shareholders.
- Normally a minimum price is stipulated, and investors subscribe for a given number of shares at a price they are prepared to pay for them.
- When the offer is closed, a strike price is determined. This will normally be set with a view to achieving an active secondary market, and all bidders at or above this price will be satisfied.

Although this form of offering is more attractive in terms of achieving the best result for the company, the administrative complications involved have made this a less popular option in practice.

Offer for Subscription

- This is rarely used now, but involves the company issuing its new shares directly to the public.
- A detailed prospectus and advertisement in a national newspaper are required for a full listing.

- An issuing house fully underwrites the issue for an agreed commission, ensuring the company sells all the shares on offer. Usually this is conditional upon the company achieving a minimum subscription level.
- This kind of IPO can also be offered on either a fixed or tender price basis.

Placing

- The company markets the issue via a broker, an issuing house or other financial institution.
- The shares are then placed to selected clients (hence the alternative term for a placing, (selective placing').
- The advantages of this method are as follows:
    ○ prospectus does not need to be so detailed.
    ○ underwriting not required.
    ○ advertising not required, unless a full listing is proposed.
    ○ as a result, this is a cheaper alternative for the company seeking a listing.

Most AIM companies will issue their shares using this method.

Intermediaries Offer

An intermediaries offer is where the issuer (or their broker) offers securities to intermediaries (eg, merchant banks) for them to then subscribe on behalf of their own clients.

5.2.4   Introduction

Companies can also achieve a listing on the London Stock Exchange by means of an introduction. These are not IPO's, since no new capital is raised. This method is available to those companies already listed on an overseas exchange or demutualised companies like former building societies. The benefit of a full listing is to make the shares more accessible to UK investors, which could aid any capital-raising activities which may be required in the future.

6.   INDICES

6.1   INTRODUCTION

Indices are a very useful way of comparing the value of a variable over different points in time.

The way they work, is to choose a point in time, known as the base period, and give the value of the variable at that time an arbitrary value. For simplicity, this is usually a round number such as 10,100 or 1,000. Future changes to the index value of the variable can then be compared with the base value or subsequent values, to indicate trends over a period of time or signal movements against the trend.

Index numbers are very useful for comparing how the value of a basket comprising many different items, changes over a period of time. These indices are called composite indices. Both the Retail Prices Index (RPI) and the Consumer Prices Index (CPI) are examples of composite indices, which indicate the level and growth (or reduction) of inflation in the UK economy.

The level of these indices will be interpreted by the market in terms of economic outlook, which may have profound implications for both bond and stock prices. In addition, there will be a tangible effect on the value and coupon of certain index-linked securities, eg, index-linked gilts.

6.2   STOCK MARKET INDICES

Stock market indices are also examples of composite indices, the main difference being that dividend income is normally added to the value of the constituents of the index, to provide an index of total return. There are over 3,000 market indices worldwide, some of which track the performance of a single market, and others which cover a sector, region or combination of markets.

Stock market indices have many uses.

1. to act as a barometer for the market;
2. to aid portfolio measurement;
3. to assist with asset allocation decisions;
4. to act as the basis for certain other investment products eg, index tracker funds, exchange traded funds, index derivative or structured products.

We will examine the use of indices in terms of portfolio performance and review in Module 7.

6.2.1   Types of Equity Index

There are many different methods of constructing an index, for example geometric, arithmetic, weighted or unweighted. We will look at the three most commonly used methods below, but before doing so, let us consider the thought processes which should be followed before constructing an index from scratch.

When considering how to construct an index, the following points should be borne in mind:

- Which markets or sectors to track.
- The basis for inclusion of its constituents.
- How to combine or average the relative prices of the various constituents.
- Whether and how to weight these constituents.
- How changes to constituents are going to be handled.
- Whether to include or exclude dividend income.

There also needs to be consideration for the potential user of the index, as follows:

- Does it satisfy the needs of investors?
- Is it taken from a broad enough base?
- Can it be replicated for portfolio performance measurement, or by product providers for index related products?
- Are there any restrictions on holding any constituents?
- Is it transparent in terms of composition and calculation?

The three most commonly used indices are as follows:

Price Weighted Arithmetic Indices

These indices assume that an equal number of shares are held in each of the constituents. It follows that those constituents with the higher share price, will have a greater impact on the overall index value, compared with those constituents with a lower share price.

Whilst this type of index is relatively easy to administer, the disadvantage of weighting in favour of the more expensive stocks, is considerable. In addition, there is no account taken of the number of shares in issue of each constituent, which may make the index unrepresentative of the true market performance.

EXAMPLE

The price of an index constituent with a high price at the base period, could fall by 50p. This could have a profound effect on the price-weighted index, even though the other constituents had all risen. In reality, the per cent fall in the high price may be minimal, and there may be so few shares of this constituent in issue, that this would, in practice, have had little effect on investors in the market, or sector as a whole. The reverse situation could also occur, where a highly-priced but small issue stock went up, dragging the index with it, disguising the fact that most of the other index constituents fell.

This makes a price-weighted arithmetic index unsuitable as a performance measurement benchmark, or as a market barometer.

 Can you think of an example of a price-weighted arithmetic index?

The Dow Jones Industrial Average (DJIA) is a price-weighted arithmetic index, and has survived despite the shortcomings highlighted above.

Unweighted Geometric Indices

With these types of index, the geometric mean is used to calculate the value of the index.

 What is the difference between arithmetic and geometric mean?

Arithmetic mean is what most people understand by the word 'average', in that a set of numbers are added, and the sum is divided by the count of numbers in the set, **n**.

The geometric mean is similar, except all the numbers in the set are multiplied and then the nth root of the product is taken.

EXAMPLE

Take two numbers, 2 and 8.

The **arithmetic mean** is 2 + 8 = 10 divided by 2 = 5

The **geometric mean** is the square root (ie, the second root) of 2 x 8 = 16 which is 4.

The disadvantages of this type of index are:

- It always understates the price rises and overstates the price falls, compared with a price weighted arithmetic index.
- It collapses if the value of a constituent falls to zero, since anything multiplied by zero is zero!

For these reasons, unweighted geometric indices should not be used to measure portfolio performance or as a market barometer.

 Can you think of an example of an unweighted geometric index?

An example of this type of index is the FT ordinary share index or FT30.

Market-Value-Weighted Arithmetic Indices

The constituents of these types of index are weighted in terms of their relative market capitalisation. In addition, the constituents are usually drawn from a broad base of the market being represented.

This makes them the more suitable for performance measurement, asset allocation and for pricing index related products. They still have a disadvantage in that if dominated by a handful of large cap companies, they may not offer the diversity needed for comparison with portfolio performance, or an index-based product.

 Can you think of an example of a market-value-weighted arithmetic index?

Examples would include the FTSE 100, S&P500 and the Hang Seng.

Free Float Indices

The 'free float' is the proportion of a company's securities available to 'outside' investors. It usually excludes shares held by strategic investors or government holdings in large privatised companies. Some overseas companies limit the amount of shares available to non-resident investors. FTSE adjust their indices according to the free float. This makes the indices more useful as a measurement of performance since it reflects more closely what fund managers can actually buy.

Capped Indices

The FSTE capped 5% index series are based on the underlying constituents of the FTSE 100 and the FTSE All-share index. Companies who have a market capitalisation of more than 5% are capped. This allows investors to monitor the impact of reducing the size of the largest companies within these two flagship indices. The FTSE All-share index is also available capped at 4%.

6.2.2 Limitations of using Equity Indices for use in Portfolio Measurement

- Do not take into account effect of costs and taxation.
- Most track price movement and do not include dividend reinvestment. Where total returns are quoted, often the dividend is assumed to be reinvested at the XD date, and not the interest payment date.
- Assume that the investor is fully invested in constituent companies at all times.
- There is a 'survivorship bias', ie, only the companies which have continued to meet the criteria of the index, remain in it, whereas other companies who have failed to meet the criteria or who have declined and then been swallowed up by other firms, will have left the index. This may not replicate the situation in a real portfolio.
- The weighting by market capitalisation often leads to a high covariance portfolio, where favoured sectors are overly represented in the index, leading to potential instability should the bubble burst.

We will look at the main stockmarket indices in greater detail in Module 7.

7. CONTRACT NOTES

The rules regarding contract notes are to be found in the FCA Handbook – Conduct of Business Sourcebook (COBS) 16.2.1R.

With the exception of where you are managing investments, for retail clients the contract note must be sent out to them 'in a durable medium' as soon as possible, and no later than the first business day following that execution.

COBS 16 Annex 1R details the information which must be included in the contract note, where applicable.

- The identification of the firm.
- The name or other designation of the client.
- The date of trade.
- The time of trade.
- Type of order (eg, limit order or market order).
- The venue identification.
- The instrument identification.
- The buy or sell indicator.
- The nature of the order if not buy or sell.
- The quantity.
- The unit price.
- The total consideration.

- The total sum of the commissions and expenses charged.
- The rate of exchange obtained (where currency conversion is required).
- The client's responsibilities in relation to settlement of the transaction (eg, time limit for payment or delivery).
- If the client's counterparty was the firm itself, in the firm's group, or another client of the firm, the fact that this was the case, unless the order was executed using a system which facilitates anonymous trading.

 Can you obtain a contract note? Look for the features we have mentioned. How does it compare with others you have seen?

COBS also states firms must retain copies of contract notes must be retained for a minimum period of five years for MiFID business, or three years for non-MiFID business.

7.1   STAMP DUTY

Stamp duty used to apply to a conveyance, transfer or a lease of land, as well as transfers on shares. Since 1 December 2003, these are now subject to stamp duty land tax.

For instruments executed on or after 1 December 2003, stamp duty only applies to transfers of stock and marketable securities, and to certain transfers of interest in partnerships.

- Tax is payable on the transfer of shares at 0.5%.
- It is usually only paid by the buyer.
- It is rounded to the nearest £5.
- It is not charged on gilts, public authority securities, UK corporate bonds, bearer stocks, transfers to registered charities and foreign registered securities.

From 13 March 2008, instruments transferring stock or marketable securities with consideration of less than £1,000, and therefore previously chargeable with £5 stamp duty, became exempt. Most do not need to be presented to HMRC for stamping, and may be sent directly to the company registrar.

7.2   STAMP DUTY RESERVE TAX (SDRT)

Stamp duty reserve tax (SDRT) was introduced in 1986 to deal with transactions in shares where a transfer form had been executed. Paperless transactions are outside the scope of stamp duty. It is a transaction tax, charged on 'agreements to transfer chargeable securities', unlike stamp duty, which is charged upon documents. The rate is also 0.5% and the same conditions listed above for stamp duty also apply to SDRT, apart from the rounding of SDRT to the nearest 1p.

SDRT now accounts for the majority of taxation collected on share transactions effected through the UK's Exchanges. The majority of this taxation is collected automatically through the CREST system, although payments are also collected for transactions that are effected outside of CREST (referred to as 'Off Market Payments), or input incorrectly through CREST. This is done either by way of a cheque or CHAPS payment. This process eliminates the need for a document, ie, stock transfer form. However, if a paper transaction is drawn up and duly stamped, the transaction will fall within the stamp duty regime, and the SDRT charge is cancelled.

7.3   PANEL ON TAKEOVERS AND MERGERS

In order to cover the running costs of the panel on takeovers and mergers (POTAM), a £1 levy is imposed on all sterling contracts of **equities**, where the consideration **exceeds £10,000**. This is imposed on both the purchases and sales.

7.4   VAT

Commission

Stockbrokers commission is exempt from VAT. The following are also exempt:

*   Unit trust annual and initial charges.
*   Commission on sale of unit trusts, life assurance and pensions.

Investment Management Fees

Are generally **subject to VAT**.

Offset Charging Schemes

Some brokers offer a scheme where they charge the client the full rate of commission (with no VAT payable), and offset these commissions against the annual management fee (which is subject to VAT). This reduces, or could even eliminate, the VAT payable by the client over the year.

7.5   NOMINEE COMPANIES

Nominee companies are formed by banks or other fiduciary organisations (one that holds assets in trust for a beneficiary). They are typically wholly-owned subsidiaries (separate legal entities) that do not trade.

Assets that are held separately from those belonging to the financial organisation, and in trust for clients, cannot be sold by a liquidator and the proceeds used to repay the firms debts, should the firm become insolvent.

Financial institutions set up nominee companies, with the sole purpose of holding client's assets separately from their own (segregating the assets) to give clients maximum protection under English law. Shares and securities owned by clients are legally registered in the name of the nominee company, (which becomes the legal owner) but the beneficial ownership remains with the client.

This aids in administering portfolios and speeds up trading.

Nominee companies maintain accounts, which may be 'designated' or 'pooled'. If a client's securities are held in a designated account, they are separately identifiable from those of the firm's other clients. If they are held in a 'pooled' account, although there will clearly be detailed records showing which clients own what, there may be one large holding registered, covering the individual holdings of a large number of underlying clients.

Given that the function of a nominee company is to register and administer holdings of shares and securities on behalf of clients, they are often involved in administrative tasks, such as:

- collection of dividends;
- preparation of annual consolidated tax vouchers;
- advising clients of corporate actions and seeking their instructions;
- arranging transfers when a share is purchased or sold.

TRUSTS AND TRUSTEES

An exam specification breakdown is provided at the back of this workbook

1. INTRODUCTION

In this section we will be examining the principles and key features of trusts and the law governing their creation and management.

Some of the terminology and concepts will already be familiar to you. We will build upon this knowledge and introduce different concepts with which you may be less familiar. We hope that this will give you confidence for your examination.

You must continue reading and extending your understanding around the topics covered, through additional study. This workbook does not represent everything you may be expected to know for the examination.

You will see icons or symbols alongside the text. These indicate activities or questions that have been designed to check your understanding and help you validate your understanding.

Here is a guide as to what each of the symbols means:

 Question

This identifies a question that will enable you to check your knowledge and understanding.

 Analyse

This gives you an opportunity to consider a question posed and compare your answers to the feedback given.

 Test

At the end of the module, you will have the opportunity to validate your learning by attempting questions which require knowledge of these topics.

1.1   OBJECTIVES

Trusts and Trust Legislation

1. Know the key features of trusts – arrangement, participants, types, documentation.
2. Know the different types of trust and what each is designed to achieve.
3. Understand the key provisions of the Trustee Act 2000 and how these relate to the investment powers of trustees, and the trust deed.

Taxation of Trusts

4. Understand the concept of a Chargeable Lifetime Transfer and be able to assess the IHT consequences of different scenarios relating to interest in possession.
5. Know the requirements for charitable status, how charities are taxed, and the purpose and rules of Gift Aid.

2. TRUSTS AND TRUST LEGISLATION

2.1 HISTORY OF TRUSTS

The law of trusts developed in the Middle Ages around the time of the Crusades. Over the centuries since the introduction of Roman law, England had developed a fairly detailed set of rules which the population was obliged to abide by. This was known as common law – common since the rules had to be adhered to by everyone.

The courts enforced common law by following decisions and principles laid down in previous cases very closely. Whilst this served a useful purpose for settling the majority of disputes, at times, the application of the rigid and inflexible rules that had developed through the courts led to problems when dealing with more unusual circumstances. In the 14th century, a system was introduced whereby anyone who found the application of common law to be unfair or 'inequitable' could apply to the King. He soon delegated his powers to the Lord Chancellor who then established the Court of Chancery. The cases brought before the Court of Chancery were not decided on common law but according to the judge's sense of justice. Over time, the law of equity evolved with its very own rules, principles and procedures.

Wealthy landowners would go away to fight for the king for several years. Rather than leave their property unoccupied, they sometimes transferred it to a relative. This was done on the strict understanding that the relative and their family could live on the land in return for looking after it, but when the wealthy landowner returned, they would have to transfer it back. As you can imagine, after many years of enjoying the property, some of these relatives reneged on their side of the deal on the return of the (formerly) wealthy landowner!

Under common law, the legal title was in the relative's name so the courts could not recognise any right to the property from the former owner. A device known as the 'use' was developed to avoid this happening. This enabled the wealthy landowner to convey the legal title to the relative but at the same time oblige him to hold the land for the use of another (the wealthy landowner in this case). Whilst this arrangement was not recognised in common law, it was a moral obligation and therefore enforced in equity by the Court of Chancery.

The use was the forerunner of the modern trust as we know it today.

2.2 WHAT IS A TRUST?

Whilst there is no statutory definition of a trust, the following summarises the key elements which should be present:

*   an **individual** (settlor);
*   gifts certain **assets** (the trust property);
*   to be managed by a **third party** (trustee);
*   in accordance with **defined objectives** (the trust deed);
*   for the benefit of **certain people** (beneficiaries).

2.3   TRUST CREATION

Trusts can be created by a variety of means including orally, by deed, by will, by statute or, as we shall see later, in secret. We will now look at the methods most commonly used by settlers, in turn:

2.3.1   Creation by Deed

This is the most common method of creating a trust. There is no prescribed format but most solicitors and trust corporations will have tried and tested templates that can easily be adapted to suit the settlor's particular requirements.

The deed will specify the following:

* the trust property;
* the names of the trustees;
* the names of the beneficiaries;
* the name of the protector (if there is one);
* the powers of the trustees;
* the rights of the beneficiaries.

It must be signed by the settlor and is usually also signed by the trustees to confirm their acceptance.

Trusts can also be created over life policies very simply, by filling out the life office's trust form.

2.3.2   Creation by Will

A trust can be expressly stated in the will or arise because of a gift to a minor. Even if the will does not include provisions to set up a trust, the executors are effectively holding the entire estate on trust for the beneficiaries until they can fully distribute it.

Clearly, a will trust will not come into operation until after the testator has died. Therefore the trust may not receive any assets until many years after the will is prepared. There is also the possibility that the will may be revoked prior to death, so the trust never comes into operation.

Some wills avoid the need and possible expense of setting up trusts, by providing permission for the parents of any minors to provide a valid receipt for property left to their children.

2.3.3   Creation by Statute

There are many trusts created or implied by statute.

The following are two examples of such trusts:

* **Section 33 Administration of Estates Act 1925** – This provides for the creation of a trust for sale on intestacy. This has been altered by Section 5 of the Trusts of Land and Appointment of Trustees Act 1996 the effect of which is that personal representatives now have a power, but not a duty, to sell land held within the estate.
* **Section 36 Law of Property Act 1925** – where a legal estate is held by two or more persons as joint tenants, it is held in trust.

2.4 LEGAL REQUIREMENTS FOR A VALID TRUST

2.4.1 The Three Certainties

In order to create a valid express trust, **three certainties** are required.

Certainty of intention – words must be used indicating an intention to create a trust. The equitable maxim 'equity looks at the intention not the form' means that no particular form of words is used but the court will look at the words used in light of all the circumstances. 'On trust for' would be sufficient in this regard.

Certainty of object – it must be clear for whom the trust is intended. This could be a simple case of naming the beneficiaries 'A & B in equal shares absolutely' or to a class of people 'any of my children who survive me'.

CASE STUDY

In a case called **McPhail v Doulton (1971)** the rule was tested thoroughly where a will included a gift to the employees of a certain company, and their relatives and dependents. The test that was put forward by the House of Lords was to ask the question 'can a trustee tell with certainty, in relation to any hypothetical individual who presents himself before the trustee, whether he is a member of that class?'

In **this** case it was possible to ascertain whether any person presenting themselves was either an employee, a relative or a dependent, so the trust was valid for certainty.

As we shall discuss later, charitable trusts need not fail for uncertainty of object.

Certainty of subject matter – it must be established, with clarity, what property is to be held on the express trust. If the subject matter is not certain, the whole trust fails (although hopefully, if the settlor is still alive, they would be able to clarify the position).

2.4.2 Rules against Perpetuities and Accumulations

It has long been considered against public policy to allow property to be retained in trust for an indefinite length of time. Similarly, it was decided in Thelluson v Woodford (1799) that if trustees were allowed to accumulate income indefinitely, then in theory, the trust fund will grow with compound interest and could eventually contain a significant proportion of the national wealth. This seems extraordinary now, but it was clearly of great concern at the time!

Please note that the perpetuity rule does not apply to gifts to charities.

The rules against **perpetuities** are contained in the Perpetuities and Accumulations Act 1964 which states that the ultimate interest in a settlement must vest within one of the following periods:

1. The lifetime of a specified person alive when the trust was created plus 21 years.
2. A fixed period of 80 years from the date the trust was created. This was increased to 125 years in the **Perpetuities and Accumulation Act 2009** but the 80-year limit still applies to trusts set up before April 2010.

The rules on accumulation of income are as follows:

Maximum Accumulation Periods

Under the Law of Property Act 1925, income may not be accumulated for longer than one of the following four periods:

1.   The life of the settlor.
2.   21 years from the death of the testator or settlor.
3.   The minority of any persons living at that time (ie, until they are 18).
4.   The minority of any persons entitled under the settlement.

A further two periods were added by the Perpetuities and Accumulations Act 1964 section 13 for trusts coming into force after 15 July 1964.

5.   The period of 21 years from the date of making the disposition.
6.   The minority of any person in being at that date.

2.4.3   Constitution of the Trust

Depending on what type of property is involved, certain formalities need to be satisfied before the property is validly transferred, and the general principle is that 'equity will not perfect an imperfect gift'. Thus, in the case of land, there needs to be a deed, and in the case of shares, Sections 182-183 of the Companies Act 1985 provides that in general, a share transfer form must be executed and delivered with the share certificates, followed by entry of the name of the new owner in the company books.

2.5   PARTIES TO A TRUST

As we have already discussed, every trust has a settlor, trustees and beneficiaries. Some trusts also have a 'protector'. We will look at each of these participants in turn.

2.5.1   Settlor

The settlor is the person who sets up the trust by transferring money or other property to trustees to hold upon the terms of the trust they are seeking to establish. The terms of the trust will be laid out in a trust deed for gifts during the settlor's lifetime (*inter vivos*) or in the will on death.

The placing of property into trust is effectively a gift of the assets, which means that the settlor no longer has any control over them. However, some settlors find this unpalatable and therefore many modern trust deeds include provisions which reserve certain powers for the settlor. Commonly the settlor will wish to reserve the power to appoint and remove trustees but they can go further and reserve the power to appoint investment managers or, more unusually, retain the investment powers completely.

On a practical point, settlors need to be careful not to retain too much control, since the courts could set aside the trust as a 'sham' in such circumstances. This would mean that the trust is ignored for tax purposes and therefore any potential tax benefits of setting up the trusts would be lost. This is far more common with offshore trusts where it may be possible for the settlor to also be a beneficiary.

Who do you think may be a settlor?

In fact, any 'legal entity' which is capable of owning or transferring property could be a settlor, which could include an individual or a corporation.

2.5.2   Trustees

The trustees are the legal owners of the trust property and on appointment the property will be vested in them by the settlor. This process is known as 'constituting the trust'.

The original trustees are appointed by the trust deed, sometimes called a 'settlement'. The original trustees of will trusts are appointed in the will. If someone dies intestate (without a valid will) the administrators will be the trustees of any trust set up as a result.

 Who do you think may be appointed a trustee?

Anyone capable of owning a legal interest in property may be appointed as a trustee, which means that they have to be over 18 and of sound mind (*sui juris*). This also includes corporate entities known as trust corporations, empowered by their memorandum and articles to act as a trustee. Most major banks have subsidiaries who perform this function eg, Barclays Bank Trust Company Ltd.

How Many Trustees are Allowed?

There can be any number of trustees although most trusts will have between two and five.

Where the trust contains land, in order to give a valid receipt for the proceeds of sale, there must be at least two trustees (unless one is a trust corporation) and no more than four.

Duties of Trustees

As we have seen, the job of the trustee is to hold the trust property for the benefit of the beneficiaries in accordance with the trust provisions.

The role carries with it the following principal general duties:

- **Comply with the terms of the trust** – the trustee must be familiar with the terms of the trust and comply with the duties and powers contained in the trust instrument. Any failure in this duty could be in breach of trust and the trustees would have to make good any losses which have arisen as a result of negligence.

- **To take control of the trust property** – the trustee must ascertain the assets of the trust and ensure these are vested in the names of the trustees. For example, they will need to make sure that any shareholdings are registered in the names of the trustees. Failure to do so could result in loss or misappropriation, which would also be a breach of trust for which the trustee would be liable.

- **Act impartially between the beneficiaries** – trustees must act in the best interests of the beneficiaries but importantly must also act impartially between all the beneficiaries. As we will discuss later, some beneficiaries only have an interest in the income arising in a trust, and others may have just an interest in the capital. When considering which investments to purchase on behalf of a trust, the trustees must have regard to the interests of all beneficiaries and not be biased one way or another. We will look at the powers of investment in greater detail later.

- **Duty to keep accounts** – a trustee must keep clear and accurate accounts of the trust, and provide them to beneficiaries on request.
- There is no duty to have these audited, but the trustee can choose to do so.

- **Duty to provide information** – a trustee must produce information and documents on request of the beneficiaries.

- **Duty of care** – in addition to the above general duties, there has always existed an overarching duty of care which covers all the actions of a trustee. Whilst this has developed over the years from common law, it has now been complimented by the statutory duty of care imposed by Part I of the Trustee Act 2000.

- **Common Law duty of care** – this has been developed from case law over the years, and interestingly (for us) most of the important cases were concerned with investment related issues.

- **Speight v Gaunt (1883)** – a trustee should conduct trust affairs in the same way a prudent man of business would conduct his own. This case centred on the use of agents, in this case a stockbroker, who defaulted on his duties. However, the trustee was not found liable since he had been prudent in seeking expert help.

- **Re Whitely (1886)** – in relation to investment, a trustee should use the same diligence as a man of ordinary prudence would take in the management of his own affairs, or the affairs of someone for whom he felt morally bound to provide.

- **Re Luckings Will Trusts (1968)** – this concerned the management of a majority interest in private company shares within a trust. A majority shareholder would be more prudent to seek further information than an ordinary shareholder, indeed he may seek a seat on the board. If he did not do so, he would be lacking in his duty of care.

- **Bartlett v Barclays Bank Trust Co Ltd (1980)** – again, this case concerned the management of a private company and the court followed the ruling in Re Luckings Will Trusts but also said that a higher duty of care is expected of a professional trustee who specialises in trust management.

- **Statutory duty of care** – the Trustee Act 2000, which came into effect on 1 February 2001, established a new statutory duty of care for trustees. This is found in Part I, which is reproduced below:
  Whenever the duty under this subsection applies to a trustee, he must exercise such care and skill as is reasonable in the circumstances, having regard in particular:
  a. to any special knowledge or experience that he has or holds himself out as having, and
  b. if he acts as trustee in the course of a business or profession, to any special knowledge or experience that it is reasonable to expect of a person acting in the course of that kind of business or profession.

As you will see, this legislation imposes a general standard of care as what a reasonable man would do in the circumstances but supports the ruling in Bartlett v Barclays Bank Trust Co Ltd for professional trustees and those with specialist knowledge or experience.

Limitations of the Statutory Duty of Care

The statutory duty of care will only apply to the following:

a. exercising the powers of investment;
b. acquisition of land;
c. using agents, nominees or custodians;
d. insurance of trust property.

Furthermore, it is possible (under Schedule 1 Section 7 of the Trustee Act 2000) to exclude the statutory duty of care in the trust instrument.

However, the common law duty of care will apply to each and every exercise of the trustees' powers, therefore it will continue to be of great relevance and importance to the activities of trustees.

Exemption Clauses

In addition to being able to exclude the statutory duty of care, trust instruments have, for some time, commonly included exemption clauses whereby the settlor agrees to exonerate the trustees from any liability for negligence. In Armitage v Nurse 1998 an exemption clause of this type was considered by the courts and it was held that exemption clauses were valid for any breach of trust in the absence of dishonesty. As you can imagine, you will not see many modern trust deeds managed by solicitors and professional trustees without this clause inserted!

Powers of Trustees

The trust deed will commonly confer additional powers to the trustees. This could be specific investment powers or, if there is a life policy held in trust, the power to pay premiums, make claims, exercise options and switch funds.

All trustees must act unanimously in the exercise of their powers.

The Trustee Act 1925 also conferred statutory powers on trustees with regard to the power to apply income (Section 31) or capital (Section 32) to beneficiaries.

Trustee Act 2000

As we shall see later, the **Trustee Act 2000** conferred new statutory powers of investment, on trustees.

In addition, this Trustee Act gave trustees a statutory **power to delegate** day-to-day duties to an agent, including the powers of investment. The Act requires the trustees to set out a policy statement stating how the investment management functions should be managed in the best interest of the trust.

The Act also created an express **professional charging clause** for non-charitable trusts which allows the payment of fees to a trustee appointed in a professional capacity, where there is no charging clause in the deed.

    What do you think the position is for laypersons acting as trustees?

The general rule is that trustees cannot benefit from their position, therefore laypersons are not allowed to charge for acting as a trustee, but can claim reasonable 'out of pocket' expenses.

The Act also gave the trustees the **power to insure** 100% of the trust property.

2.5.3   Beneficiaries

The beneficiaries are the persons or objects for whose benefit the trust is created. Beneficiaries can either be named in the trust instrument ('my children Jenny and Sarah in equal shares') or described by a class ('all my children in equal shares'). Clearly the latter approach would provide extra flexibility if a settlor was intending to have more children. In certain cases, the trustees may be given the power to exercise discretion as to who benefits from the trust.

There are various types of beneficial interest:

Absolute vested interest – the beneficiary has a full equitable ownership, which cannot be taken away. There are three conditions which must be satisfied for an interest to be vested:

1. the identity of the beneficiary is known, and
2. any conditions are satisfied, and
3. the respective shares are known.

If any of these conditions is not satisfied, the interest is known as a **contingent interest**.

Life interest – a beneficiary (called the life tenant) is entitled to the income on the trust property but not the capital. An immediate right to the income is called an **interest in possession**. Where there are successive life interests, the person who is not enjoying the immediate right to the income has an **interest in remainder**.

Remaindermen – these beneficiaries will receive the capital of the trust fund on the death of the life tenant. Until that time their interest is known as an **interest in reversion (or reversionary interest)**.

EXAMPLE

Dave settles money on Julia for life then to Phillippa for life and then to Freddie provided he attains 21 (he is four at present).

Julia – has an interest in possession – which is vested.

Phillippa – has an interest in remainder – which is vested since there are no conditions.

Freddie - has an interest in reversion – which is contingent on him attaining 21.

A beneficiary cannot control the trustees but they do have a personal right to enforce the trust and ensure that the trustees carry out its provisions.

In certain circumstances the beneficiaries can terminate the trust.

This is known as the rule in **Saunders v Vautier 1841**. The following conditions must be present for them to successfully call for an end to the trust:

1. all the beneficiaries are ascertained, and
2. there is no possibility of further beneficiaries, and
3. they are all of full age and capacity, and
4. the beneficiaries are unanimous.

This rule can be expressly excluded in the trust instrument.

2.5.4 Protector

Protectors are much more common in offshore trusts than in England and Wales, and their most common role is to veto the proposals of trustees. Unlike trustees, they do not have trust property vested in their name.

The scope of the protectors powers are set out in the trust instrument and these can be either reactive or proactive.

Reactive – the protector reacts to the actions of a trustee, eg, to distribute money to a beneficiary.

Proactive – the protector takes the initiative and instigates an action, eg, to remove a trustee.

Like trustees, anyone who is *sui juris* can be a protector, including a corporate body.

PRACTICAL POINT

Clearly, the more power given to the protector, the more cumbersome the administration of the trust could become. However, appointing a protector may give the settlor the desired peace of mind that someone will be able to oversee the activities of the trustees, hence the term often used to describe this role is 'settlor's comfort'.

2.6   CLASSIFICATION OF TRUSTS

As we have seen, equity developed the law of trusts. As you would imagine, down the years many different and difficult situations have arisen requiring the court to recognise and deal with them appropriately. This has left us with many different types of trust, which are recognised by the courts as discussed below.

Express Trust

An express trust is one where the terms are expressly set out, usually in writing but for personal property this could be by a clear declaration. This could be by way of a lifetime settlement, by will or on intestacy. In the latter case this is also known as a statutory trust.

Implied Trusts

Implied trusts are created as a result of what the law infers as being a person's intention. There are two main types of implied trusts, resulting and constructive.

Resulting Trust

An implied resulting trust could arise following a transfer of property from A to B without any indication that a gift was intended or has taken place. The property would be held on a resulting trust for A, as on B's death the property would revert (be transferred back) to A. Similarly, A could transfer property to B to hold for C's lifetime. If there is no instruction as to what is to happen to that property on C's death the property would be held on a resulting trust for A, as on C's death the property would return to A (or A's estate if he too had died).

Constructive Trust

A constructive trust is one that is imposed by law, usually to remedy inequitable, unconscionable, improper or unjust conduct. An example would be where someone acts as trustee 'de son tort' ie, that he acts as though he is a trustee and receives an item of trust property or makes a profit at the expense of a trust. In these circumstances he is legally deemed to be holding the property and profit on constructive trusts for the benefit of the beneficiaries and is accountable to them for it.

Another example of where a constructive trust will be imposed is where there is a **secret trust**.

EXAMPLE

More about secret trusts (because everybody loves a secret)

These trusts take effect though the operation of the will. The intention of a secret trust is to obtain confidentiality. The beneficiaries, and the terms of the trust, can remain secret. There are strict rules, which must be followed in order for these trusts to be valid. There are fully secret trusts and half secret trusts.

With fully secret trusts, the will may appear to leave property absolutely to individual **A**. However, at some point during their lifetime, the testator must have communicated either orally or in writing (or by sealed letter to be opened upon the testator's death) with **A**, who agreed to hold the property in trust for another or others.

Half secret trusts are where the trust is partially expressed in the will. The word trust can appear in the will but not the terms of the trust or the intended beneficiaries. The purpose of these trusts is again to retain confidentiality but also to prevent possible fraud by the 'legatee'. An example of such a trust would be 'to Jayne on the terms I have previously communicated to her'. The rule with regard to the communication of half secret trusts is different to that of fully secret trusts in that the communication (written or oral) and acceptance, must take place either before or at the same time as making the will.

Automatic Resulting Trust

Automatic resulting trusts also arise through the operation of law.

Where one person transfers property or funds to another for a specific purpose, this creates a trust relationship between them. The recipient is under an obligation to carry out that purpose.

EXAMPLE OF AN AUTOMATIC RESULTING TRUST

In **Barclays Bank Ltd v Quistclose Investments Ltd 1970**, Rolls Razor was deeply indebted to Barclays. It needed further additional sums to be able to pay a dividend which it had declared. Rolls Razor borrowed funds from Quistclose in order to satisfy the dividend declared. The terms of the loan were such that the funds would only be used for the sole purpose of paying the dividend. The loan was paid into an account with Barclays, and Barclays was given notice of the arrangement.

However, between the time that the loan was advanced and the dividend being paid, Rolls Razor went into liquidation. Barclays Bank claimed that they were entitled to exercise a set-off of the money in the account against the debts that Rolls Razor owed to Barclays. Quistclose claimed that the moneys had to be returned to them, as the purpose for which they had been lent had now failed and were incapable of being fulfilled (as Rolls Razor was now in liquidation).

The House of Lords (with the leading judgment being given by Lord Wilberforce) unanimously held that the money was held by Rolls Razor on trust for the payment of the dividends; that purpose having failed, the money was held on trust for Quistclose. The fact that the transaction was a loan, did not exclude the implication of a trust. The legal rights (to call for repayment) and equitable rights (to claim title) could co-exist. Barclays, having notice of the trust, could not claim the money to set off against the debts of Quistclose. Similarly, the liquidator of Rolls Razor could not claim title to the money, as the assets did not form part the beneficial estate of Rolls Razor. This was a landmark case and henceforth, these types of trusts are often described as **Quistclose Trusts**.

This ruling was backed up Lord Millet in a later case which went to the House of Lords, namely **Twinsectra v Yardley 2002**.

3.   TYPES OF TRUST

We will discuss the taxation aspects of the most commonly used trusts later, but in the meantime let us consider the main features, benefits and possible uses of the following trusts.

3.1   BARE TRUST

A bare trust is where the trustee holds the trust property for a single beneficiary who is of full age and mental capacity. The beneficiary, who holds the whole of the equitable interest may, under Saunders v Vautier (1841), call for the legal interest from the trustee which will give them absolute ownership property held in trust, and therefore end the trust.

One example of this would be a life policy on trust for Jimmy (an adult) absolutely. In this case, the trustee's duty is just to claim the proceeds from the life office and pay it over to Jimmy.

 In what circumstances do you think bare trusts would be an appropriate solution?

Bare trusts are particularly useful for grandparents who wish to pass on assets to their grandchildren or set aside money for their school fees or university education. As we discussed earlier, the named beneficiary has an 'absolute entitlement' to the assets that are placed in trust, but they will be held in the name of the trustee until the child reaches the age of 18.

This could be useful for settling assets which the beneficiary could not hold directly, for example stocks and shares (because minors cannot contract to buy and sell them).

On reaching age 18, the beneficiary will be able to call on the assets. The trustees will have no discretion over whether to comply with this request. As we shall see later, the income on a bare trust is deemed to be that of the beneficiary who will be able to use any unused personal allowance to mitigate, or avoid completely, any income tax on the income arising within the trust fund. For parents, this type of trust is not so attractive, since any income over £100 would be deemed to be that of the parents, for income tax purposes. For grandparents however, this rule does not apply.

Any growth on the assets held in trust will be outside the estate of the settlor and, provided the settlor survives seven years from the date of creating the trust, there will be no inheritance tax to pay.

The disadvantage of bare trusts is the lack of flexibility – the beneficiary can get his or her hands on the funds at 18, which may not be desirable (for the settlor!).

3.2   INTEREST IN POSSESSION TRUST

An interest in possession is the right to receive an income from the trust fund, or use of the trust assets.

Interests in possession are sometimes established in a will, and are a potentially useful way of providing a safe income for dependants of the settlor, whilst ensuring that some assets are saved in order to be passed on at a later date.

New legislation enacted in 2006 changed the tax treatment of these trusts, and new interest in possession trusts are now treated in much the same way as discretionary trusts, for inheritance tax purposes. As such, whilst an interest in possession trust may well still be a viable option, some settlors will wish to investigate other possibilities, particularly discretionary trusts which provide greater flexibility.

3.2.1   Power of Appointment (or Flexible) Trusts

Trusts can be fixed interest trusts in as much as once they are set up, the beneficial interests cannot normally be altered. However, it is also possible to set up a trust where the trustees are given a 'power of appointment' to appoint or vary beneficiaries or vary the terms of the trust.

The class of potential beneficiaries can be drafted very widely, giving the trustees maximum flexibility. This can cater for any changing family or personal circumstances like marriage breakdowns or bankruptcy.

There will be a default beneficiary who has a right to the income (ie, an interest in possession) and possibly capital if the trustees do not make an appointment to any of the other beneficiaries.

Can you think of a situation where this arrangement could be particularly useful?

These types of trust are commonly used for life assurance policies written in trust. This gives the settlor power to change beneficial interest and appoint new trustees during his/her lifetime.

There are, of course, other advantages in setting up a life policy under a trust. These are:

*   the proceeds are, subject to certain conditions, paid outside of the deceased's estate and therefore avoid any potential inheritance tax charge;
*   the trust funds can be paid to the trustees without the need for Grant of Representation (outside probate). This means that the proceeds can be paid by the insurance company within a matter of days after production of the death certificate.

3.3   DISCRETIONARY TRUST

Discretionary trusts, along with bare trusts have become the family trust of choice. In a discretionary trust, no beneficiary has a right to the income – the trustees have the power to accumulate, and distributions will be at their discretion.

The trustees have discretion in two ways:

1. They can select which beneficiary or beneficiaries from a 'class' of beneficiaries receive payments of either income or capital.
2. They can decide the amount of trust income or capital each beneficiary receives.

An example would be 'on trust for such of my children or grandchildren as the trustees shall, from time to time, appoint'.

 What do you think are the potential uses of a discretionary trust?

The surviving spouse can be included as one of the beneficiaries of the trust. Before the ability to transfer unused inheritance tax nil-rate bands, this was a popular way of using the nil-rate band on the first death rather than simply transferring all the assets to the spouse absolutely. Although that benefit is now not so attractive, there are still many circumstances when a discretionary trust will be desirable.

For example, a discretionary trust could be appropriate where the value of the assets placed in trust is likely to grow at a faster rate than the nil-rate band. It may also be useful to take advantage of current legislation regarding business property relief or agricultural property relief.

However, the main advantage of discretionary trusts is their flexibility. Again, this can cater for changes in circumstances like possible future divorce of a child, remarriage of the surviving spouse, or the threat of bankruptcy to any beneficiary. Discretionary trusts are also useful to guard against spendthrift beneficiaries who will not be able to have access to the capital and will only benefit from the income, if the trustees so decide. Placing funds in a discretionary trust can also mean that potential beneficiaries can continue to receive means-tested benefits, which would otherwise cease. For example, this type of trust could prove very useful for providing for beneficiaries who have learning difficulties.

The settlor can guide the trustees, normally by leaving a 'letter of wishes' with the will. Although not binding, this could be a useful steer for the trustees in exercising their discretion during the lifetime of the trust.

There are certain inheritance tax disadvantages of discretionary trusts, although as we shall see later, since 22 March 2006, these are now shared with interest in possession trusts created after that date. Clearly these taxation implications need to be weighed up against the benefits of greater flexibility and control.

3.4   ACCUMULATION AND MAINTENANCE TRUST

These were a special type of discretionary trust, which were popular due to their beneficial inheritance tax treatment.

Following the Finance Act 2006, no new accumulation and maintenance trusts can be set up and any existing trusts had to make a decision as to whether to change to another type of trust in order to avoid the more onerous inheritance tax regime.

3.5   CHARITABLE TRUST

Charitable trusts are a type of **purpose trust** in that it promotes a purpose and does not primarily benefit specific individuals. In the UK, charitable trusts are regulated by the Charities Commission.

A charitable trust must be of a charitable nature, for the public benefit and wholly and exclusively **charitable**. For tax purposes, HMRC states that the definition of a 'charitable trust' is a trust established for charitable purposes only.

A charitable purpose used to be defined as:

1. The relief of poverty;
2. The advancement of education;
3. The advancement of religion;
4. Other purposes beneficial to the community.

The Charities Act 2006 replaced the above four categories and introduced 13 new purposes.

1. The prevention or relief of poverty.
2. The advancement of education.
3. The advancement of religion.
4. The advancement of health or the saving of lives.
5. The advancement of citizenship or community development.

6. The advancement of the arts, culture, heritage or science.
7. The advancement of amateur sport.
8. The advancement of human rights, conflict resolution or reconciliation or the promotion of religious or racial harmony or equality and diversity.
9. The advancement of environmental protection or improvement.
10. The relief of those in need, by reason of youth, age, ill-health, disability, financial hardship or other disadvantage.
11. The advancement of animal welfare.
12. The promotion of the efficiency of the armed forces of the Crown; or the efficiency of the police, fire and rescue services or ambulance services.
13. Any other purposes charitable in law.

In fact the purposes defined in the Charities Act 2006 are very similar to those used previously, but with greater detail on what constitutes 'other purposes beneficial for the community'. The last category meant that everything which was previously considered charitable, remained so.

Prospective charities must apply to the Charity Commission to claim charitable status and thereby the tax benefits connected with a charity.

3.5.1   The Benefits of Being a Charitable Trust

Generally speaking, charitable trusts are subject to the same rules as private trusts, but they enjoy a number of advantages over private trusts, some of which are particularly relevant when considering the management of investments on behalf of the Trustees.

The Perpetuity Rule

We discussed earlier that the perpetuity rule prohibits settlors from tying up their property indefinitely. Charitable trusts are the exception to this rule, since they will be valid even though they may last for an infinite period of time.

Tax Advantages

As you would expect, charitable trusts and charities enjoy significant tax advantages, and this is the main motivation for bodies seeking charitable status.

The investments of charities are:

- exempt from income tax;
- exempt from capital gains tax on disposals by the trust;
- exempt from stamp duty.

In addition:

- no capital gains tax is payable on gifts by individuals to charity (this is an exempt disposal);
- no inheritance tax is payable on outright gifts by individuals, to a charity;
- charities benefit from a mandatory 80% business rate relief for the premises that they occupy. The further 20% is discretionary and may be awarded by the local authority to whom the rates are payable;
- gifts to charitable trusts may qualify for income tax relief under gift aid (or a payroll-giving scheme) as described in the following section.

3.5.2   Gift Aid

Gift aid is basically tax relief on money donated to UK and EU (plus Norway and Iceland) charities and community amateur sports clubs.

HMRC treat donations as if the donor had already deducted basic-rate tax from them. The charity can then reclaim this tax, to increase the value of a donation.

The original Gift Aid Scheme was introduced in 1990. It enabled UK resident individuals and companies to give single gifts of money to charity tax-effectively, but it required a minimum amount (£250) to be given.

The Gift Aid scheme was amended by Finance Act 2000, for donations made by individuals on or after 6th April 2000. This abolished the £250 minimum limit for Gift Aid donations, so the scheme now applies to any donation, whether large or small, regular or one-off.

How it Works

Charities take the donation, which is money that has already been taxed - and reclaim basic rate tax from HM Revenue & Customs (HMRC) on its 'gross' equivalent - the amount before basic-rate tax was deducted.

Basic-rate tax is 20%, so this means that a gift of £10 using Gift Aid is worth £12.50 to the charity.

Higher-rate taxpayers can claim the difference between the higher rate of tax (40% and the basic rate of tax (20%) on the total (gross) value of the donation to the charity, on their self-assessment forms.

EXAMPLE

Peter is a higher-rate taxpayer. He donates £100, but the total value of his donation to the charity is £125. In addition, he can claim back 20% of this (£25) for himself. He will need to make this claim via his self-assessment tax return.

Gift Aid Rules

To satisfy the Gift Aid conditions donors must:

- pay enough UK income tax and/or capital gains tax themselves to cover the amount of tax the charity will reclaim;
- give the charity a gift aid declaration, which should include:
  - their name;
  - their home address;
  - the charity's name;
  - details of the donation, stating that it is a gift aid donation;
  - confirmation that they have paid UK tax – to cover the tax the charity will reclaim.

A declaration can be made to cover individual donations, a series of donations, and can cover donations made during a specified period or to cover all future donations. They can also be backdated for up to 6 years prior to the date of the declaration, provided the donation was made since 6 April 2000.

3.5.3   Limitations of Becoming a Charity

There are restrictions on what charities can do. These are determined by the Charities Commission both in terms of purpose and operations. This is primarily to ensure that all money raised, and any surpluses, can only be distributed in accordance with the charitable objectives of the organisation. It is essential to think carefully before applying to become a registered charity.

* Charity trustees cannot be paid, other than reasonable expenses. This could restrict the professional assistance the organisation might otherwise be able to engage.
* Charity law also demands that trustees avoid any situation where charitable and personal interests might conflict.
* Charities aren't allowed to undertake political campaigning.
* Being a charity restricts the type of trading activities the organisation is allowed to undertake.

4.   THE INVESTMENT OF TRUSTS

4.1   INVESTMENT DUTIES IN EQUITY

Case law through the years has provided a clear framework as to what is expected in equity.

Trustees are expected to conduct investment business to the standard of a prudent person in business. Where the trustee is a trust corporation, that company owes a higher standard of care (Bartlett v Barclays Bank Trust Company Ltd 1980).

In Nestle v National Westminster Bank plc (1993), the court had to decide upon the balance the trustee has to achieve, as regards the interests of the life tenant and the remaindermen.

This led to some general guidelines:

1. It was not a wise policy to change investments too frequently.
2. A trustee with power of investment, should undertake periodic reviews of the investments held in trust. These reviews should be undertaken at least annually.

4.2   INVESTMENT POWERS IN THE TRUST DEED

The trustees must observe the powers granted in the trust deed. The trustees must ensure that they understand the meaning of the powers, and conform to them strictly.

Modern trust deeds often confer wide powers of investment on the trustees, for example 'invest as if absolutely entitled'. The trust deed could also give permission to retain hazardous or wasting assets. However many old trust deeds do not confer any powers of investment on trustees. In the absence of investment powers in the trust instrument, the trustee will have to rely on the investment powers laid down by statute.

4.3   STATUTORY INVESTMENT POWERS

The Trustee Investment Act 1961 defined three ranges of investment which limited the proportion of a trust that could be invested into different types of investment. The two limited and risk-adverse ranges were both known as the 'narrow range' which were essentially fixed interest securities. The riskier investments were known as 'wide range investments' which were primarily equities. The Act laid down strict rules as to the percentage split of the portfolio with regard to these ranges. If the trustees had power to retain assets, there was also a special fund in which these assets were held until disposal.

Although, at the time, this was welcome legislation, it has been found to be too restrictive in the modern era of portfolio management. The Trustee Investment Act 1961 has now been repealed in the most part, and replaced by the Trustee Act 2000.

As we have already seen, Part 1 of this Act introduced a statutory duty of care for trustees.

However, the most important aspect of this legislation, from our perspective, was contained in Part 2 of the Act. This detailed a new power of investment which is summarised as follows:

- Trustees now have the right to invest in anything as if they were 'absolutely entitled', subject to the 'standard investment criteria'.
- Standard investment criteria includes:
  - the suitability of the type of investment for the type of trust (eg, age of beneficiaries, life tenancy etc);
  - whether the particular investment selected is the most suitable of its type. The assessment of suitability will include considerations as to the size and risk of the investment, the balance between income and capital growth, and will include any relevant ethical considerations as to the kind of investments appropriate for the trust.
- The standard investment criteria cannot be excluded by a settlor in the trust instrument or by including wide powers of investment in the trust instrument.
- There is a need to review investments from time to time to see if they need to be varied. Although the act does not stipulate how frequently this must take place, the case of Nestle v National Westminster Bank plc must be borne in mind.
- There is also a need to diversify the investments of the trust in so far as it is appropriate to the circumstances of the trust
- Trustees are permitted to invest in freehold or leasehold land in the UK (but not overseas). Under the Trustee Investment Act 1961, there was a minimum unexpired term of 60 years for leasehold property, but this has been removed. Property can be bought for:
  - investment,
  - occupation by the beneficiary,
  - or for any other reason.
- Since the trustees have powers of an absolute owner, they will also have the power to mortgage.
- A trustee must seek advice before setting up a trust fund, or on review, unless the trustee does not think it is necessary in the circumstances (not defined in the act but is considered to cover situations where there are only small sums to invest). The advice must be from a person who the trustee reasonably believes to be qualified. This duty to seek advice also applies to express powers given in the trust instrument, not just the statutory investment powers.
- Trustees are also bound by their duty of care, to act fairly between all beneficiaries entitled to income and capital.
- The general power of investment does not apply to pension trusts, authorised unit trusts or certain charitable trusts.

5.   THE TAXATION OF TRUSTS

5.1   INCOME TAX

Trustees are subject to tax under self-assessment, in a similar way to the self-employed.

They need to complete annual tax returns and have to make interim payments on account as follows:

*   31 January in the year of assessment – **first payment on account** - 50% of the previous year's tax liability.
*   31 July in the following year – **second payment on account** - 50% of the previous year's tax liability.
*   31 January in the following year – **balancing payment** - for income tax and any capital gains tax payable.

All trustees are jointly liable for any outstanding tax, and are personally liable for any penalties which may be incurred.

The income tax treatment of trusts varies depending upon the circumstances and nature of the trust.

5.1.1   Income Tax Payable by the Settlor

There are certain occasions when, no matter what type of trust (other than trust for 'vulnerable' beneficiaries which includes disabled persons and bereaved minors), the income is deemed to be that of the settlor and is taxed accordingly (even though it may not have been distributed to him).

This applies in two circumstances:

*   When either the settlor, their spouse or civil partner retains an interest in the trust (but this does not include widow, widower or separated spouse or equivalent for a civil partner).
*   Where the trust is for the benefit of a minor unmarried child of the settlor.

The settlor can reclaim any tax payable on trust income from the trust, but since the rate of tax is likely to be higher than that paid in the trust, it is not good tax planning for this situation to arise.

We will look at each of the main types of trust in turn.

5.1.2   Bare Trusts

Income arising within the trust is deemed to be that of the beneficiary, who must include it in his self-assessment forms and pay tax on it personally. He will be able to use his personal allowance against this income.

5.1.3   Interest in Possession Trusts

In these types of trust, the beneficiary will have a right to the income as and when it arises.

Tax is payable within the trust, on income, at the same rates as for an individual paying basic-rate tax, ie, 20% for savings income, 10% on grossed-up dividend income and 20% on other income. However, the trust is not entitled to a personal allowance.

There is no higher-rate tax within the trust, although the beneficiary may be liable to additional tax on receipt of trust income, if this takes the beneficiary into the higher-rate band.

The beneficiary will receive a tax voucher showing the net income after expenses, and this will be broken down into the sources of income ie, savings, dividends and other income. Management expenses do not reduce the tax payable by the trustees, but may reduce the higher-rate tax payable, since they are deducted from the income to be declared by the beneficiary.

Income Tax Payable by the Beneficiary

Non-taxpayer	10% taxpayer	Basic-rate taxpayer	Higher and Additional-rate taxpayer
Can reclaim some or all of the savings or non-dividend income.	Can reclaim some of the savings income tax if this falls in the 10% band (would be very unlikely).	No further tax to pay.	Further liability will arise at the appropriate rates, less the tax deducted.

In view of the above, trustees will often mandate the income directly to the beneficiary.

5.1.4   Discretionary Trusts and Accumulation and Maintenance Trusts

- There is a standard-rate band which attracts tax at 10% or 20% depending on its source.
- This applies to the first £1,000 of income, but this amount is divided by the number of trusts created by the settlor, which were in existence in that tax year, to a minimum of £200 (for five or more trusts).
- Tax is payable at the 'trust rate', 45% from 2013–14 on income over the standard-rate band on non-dividend income, and 37.5% on dividend income. After tax deducted at source, this would leave an additional 25% payable on savings income and 27.5% on grossed-up dividends.
- Tax relief is given on certain allowable expenses, to be set against income (but not investment adviser's fees which must be charged to capital).

If income is accumulated (not paid out), then there is no further tax to pay. However, if income from a discretionary trust is distributed, it carries a 45% tax credit irrespective of the source of that income in the trust (dividend or savings income).

Non-taxpayer	Basic-rate taxpayer	Higher-rate taxpayer or Additional-rate taxpayer
Can reclaim some or all of the tax suffered.	Can reclaim 25% of the income falling within the basic-rate band.	No further tax to pay.

This can result in a further charge to income tax on the trustees. This is because they will have paid less tax to HMRC than the 45% tax they are vouching to the beneficiary (as a result of operation of the 10% standard-rate band, along with the fact there may be dividend income taxed at 37.5%). Since they are providing a tax voucher potentially enabling a beneficiary to reclaim 45% tax (if he is a non-taxpayer), HMRC could be out of pocket. To avoid this situation occurring, the trustees have to pay the extra tax from the trust, when income is distributed. They cannot use the tax withheld on dividends to reduce the tax payable in this instance, since it is not reclaimable.

EXAMPLE

Dividend received of £1800. Grossed up this is £2,000

Trustees will have to pay tax as follows:	£1,000 @ 10%	= £100
	£1,000 @ 37.5%	= £375
	Total	= £475
	Less the tax credit of £200	= £275

If they accumulate the income they will have £1,800 – £375 = £1,525

If they wanted to distribute all the income, they could only pay out £990 to the beneficiary, since they would have to give him a tax voucher for the grossed up amount and show tax deducted at 45%.

This would be a gross payment of £1,800 and tax of 810 and a net payment of £990.

Since the trustees have only paid tax of £275 to HMRC, they would have to pay an additional £535 (they can't use the tax credit in this instance, since it is not reclaimable).

This means that they would only have £1,525 less £535 = £990 available to pay out.

Clearly, in the above circumstances the danger is that the trustees could inadvertently overdraw the income account if they were not careful, and therefore they must keep a close eye on this situation. In case you were wondering, any tax on accumulated income goes into a 'tax pool' which they can carry forward to 'frank' the 45% tax credit in future years.

5.2   CAPITAL GAINS TAX (CGT)

Capital gains tax is assessed on the trustees of UK resident trusts in a very similar way to that of individuals who are basic-rate taxpayers (already covered in Module 2 of your studies). Tax payable by trustees increased from 18% to a single rate of 28% (equivalent to that for higher-rate taxpayers) on gains realised from 23 June 2010. This applies irrespective of the income of the trust or beneficiaries, except for bare trusts. Tax is due by 31 January in the year following the end of the tax year of disposal.

However, there are a few notable differences when dealing with trusts:

5.2.1   Annual Exemption

The normal CGT annual exemption available for trustees is half of that available to an individual. For 2013–14, this is therefore £5,450.

However, the trust exemption has to be shared between any trusts set up by the settlor since 6 June 1978, to a minimum of one fifth per trust.

> **Warning**
>
> **Care must be taken here, since the settlor may have a personal pension or a life policy set up in trust which he must include, even if these trusts cannot give rise to a CGT liability. However, occupational pension schemes and former retirement annuities are not included.**

Trusts for disabled persons (when the trusts for the vulnerable tax treatment is not applicable) are entitled to the same annual allowance as an individual, ie, £10,900 for 2013–14.

2013–14 Annual Exemption Amounts for Trusts

To summarise, this is how much each trust would be entitled to, where there has been more than one trust set up by the same settlor since 6 June 1978.

One Trust	Two Trusts	Three Trusts	Four Trusts	Five Trusts or more	Trust for the disabled
£5,450	£2,725 each	£1,817 each	£1,363 each	£1,090 each	£10,900

5.2.2   Holdover Relief

The creation of a trust by the settlor is a disposal for CGT purposes and the market value of the assets at the date of creation of the trust will be used to calculate the amount of any gains payable by the settlor. However, it may be possible to claim holdover relief to avoid a potential tax liability arising at that time.

Holdover relief is a form of CGT deferral where the donor of gifts of certain assets can effectively hold over the gain so that no CGT becomes payable at the time of the gift, but the acquisition cost of the receiver is reduced by the amount of the held over gain. This means that the receiver acquires the assets at the original acquisition cost to the donor. This relief has to be claimed jointly and only applied to certain assets.

In addition to outright gifts, this relief was also available for transfers into most trusts prior to **22 March 2006**.

From **22 March 2006** onwards, holdover relief is available under most circumstances, for **any assets** placed into trust. In this case, only the settlor would need to claim the relief and advise the trustees accordingly.

> **Warning**
>
> **This relief will not be available for bare trusts or trusts which include a minor unmarried child of the settlor (unless this is a trust for a disabled person). Since 9 December 2003, holdover relief has not been available for transfers into a trust, where the settlor, their spouse or civil partner has or may acquire an interest. If this relief is given, and within the clawback period (a period of six years from the end of the year of assessment in which the trust is set up) the settlor either obtains an interest or makes arrangements to obtain an interest at a later date, the relief can be clawed back by HMRC.**

In addition, holdover relief may be claimed when trustees transfer assets to beneficiaries. Under these circumstances, the relief must be claimed jointly by the beneficiaries and the trustees. The beneficiaries will effectively acquire the assets at the trustees' acquisition cost, which may enable them to defer the disposal to use their individual annual exemption or partially dispose of the assets each year, again using their individual annual exemptions, to potentially avoid a CGT charge altogether.

5.2.3   Deemed Disposals

In addition to actual disposals within the trust, a charge to CGT may also arise on other occasions within a trust. An example of this would be where an interest in possession ends on the death of a life tenant, and the property passes to the remainderman. For pre 22 March 2006 trusts, since CGT does not generally become payable on death, this often results in a free uplift of values.

> **Warning**
>
> **Where holdover relief was claimed by the settlor when transferring assets into the trust, these held over gains would normally be chargeable to CGT on the death of the life tenant. Also, if the end of the life tenancy occurred as a result of an action other than death, for example remarriage of the settlor's wife, this would be a deemed disposal by the trustees, and chargeable to CGT.**
>
> **For lifetime trusts created on or after 22 March 2006, there is generally no CGT uplift on the death of the life tenant.**

Another example of a deemed disposal is where a beneficiary becomes absolutely entitled to trust property on achieving a contingency eg, 21st birthday. Once the beneficiary has become absolutely entitled, the trustees will be holding the assets as bare trustees.

It may be helpful to consider each of the main types of trust in turn.

5.2.4   Bare Trusts

Any gains are treated as the beneficiary's gains and any liability will be payable by them. Any subsequent transfer of assets to the beneficiary will be disregarded for CGT purposes.

EXAMPLE

Blair sets up a trust under which his son Ian is entitled to the trust property if he reaches age 21. The assets are quoted shares. On 19 August 2012, Ian reaches 21 so the trustees are treated as having made a disposal for CGT purposes. They retain the shares, then sell half of the holding on 21 January 2013. This is a disposal by Ian, based on his acquisition cost as at 19 August 2012. The trustees then transfer the other half of the holding to Ian on 20 July 2013. This is ignored, and Ian's acquisition cost of these shares will again be the value as at 19 August 2012.

NB: Holdover relief could have been claimed on Ian's 21st birthday, to avoid the CGT charge at that time. This would have the effect of increasing the gain on the disposal in January 2013, and reducing the acquisition cost of the shares retained by Ian, thereby increasing any gain on a subsequent disposal.

Bare trusts for minors continue to have capital gains tax advantages, even if the trust was set up by a parent. Unlike other forms of trust, the gains on bare trusts for minors, where the parent has settled the assets, are chargeable to the minor, not the parent. This means that they will have their full annual exemption available and not the lower trust annual exemption. They are also less likely than the settlor, to need their annual exemption for other purposes.

5.2.5   Interest in Possession Trusts

To summarise what was discussed above, the position on the death of a life tenant is as follows:

Pre 22nd March 2006 Trusts

- No CGT on death of life tenant – free uplift in acquisition values.
- Held over gains are chargeable on the death of the life tenant.

EXAMPLE

Jimmy created an Interest in Possession Trust in 1994 with an asset which he had owned for 20 years, valued at £100,000. The value of the asset at 31 March 1982 was £50,000. The gain of £50,000 was held over to the trustees.

The life tenant dies on 21 January 2013 and the asset is worth £300,000 at that date.

The gain of £200,000 will not be chargeable to CGT, but the trustees will now be liable for the held over gain of £50,000.

Trusts commencing on or after 22 March 2006

- No CGT on death of life tenant – no uplift in acquisition values.
- Held over gains are chargeable on the death of the life tenant.

In addition, if the trustees allow a beneficiary to occupy a property held in the trust for their main residence, it should be possible to claim principal private residence exemption provided holdover relief was not claimed when the property was placed in trust.

5.2.6   Discretionary Trusts

Pre 22 March 2006 Trusts

- Holdover relief could be claimed by the Settlor for business assets or family company shares only.

Trusts commencing on or after 22nd March 2006

- Holdover relief can be claimed by the Settlor for all assets.
- Holdover relief is not available where the settlor has, or may acquire, an interest.
- Transfers to beneficiaries are deemed disposals for CGT purposes.

5.2.7   Accumulation and Maintenance Trusts

- There is a deemed disposal when the beneficiary becomes absolutely entitled to the trust assets - this will normally be on attaining a specified age.
- Holdover relief may be claimed – trustees and beneficiary must claim jointly.

5.3   INHERITANCE TAX

The Finance Act of 2006 drastically changed the tax treatment of trusts.

The creation of a trust is a transfer of value for IHT purposes: the amount of the gift will be assessed as the reduction in the value of the donor's estate, not necessarily the market value.

Once again, we will look at the main types of trust and consider the inheritance tax implications of each one in turn.

5.3.1   Bare Trusts

- The creation of a bare trust is a potentially exempt transfer (PET).
- The trust will only be taxable if the settlor dies within seven years.
- If the beneficiary dies, the trust will be included in his estate for inheritance tax purposes.

5.3.2   Interest in Possession Trusts

Pre 22 March 2006 Trusts

- The creation of a lifetime settlement was a PET.
- The trust was only liable for IHT if the settlor died within seven years.

Trusts created from 22 March 2006 onwards

- The creation of an interest in possession trust on or after 22 March 2006 is normally a chargeable lifetime transfer incurring tax at 20% of anything above the nil-rate band.
- If the settlor dies within seven years, there may be further tax to pay (although taper relief may be available from years three to seven).
- After seven years of the date of creation, the trust will then fall outside of the estate of the settlor, and would not be subject to tax on his or her death, unless there had been a reservation of benefit.
- Where there is a life tenant, that person would have the interest in possession.
- Where the trust is flexible (ie, the trustees have power of appointment over the funds), the default beneficiary will have the interest in possession until the trustees make an appointment.
- The trust will now be subject to periodic and exit charges with two exceptions:
  - disabled persons trusts; and
  - 'immediate post death interest' in possession trusts ie, created by will or intestacy.
- The application of periodic and exit charges is explained below.

5.3.3   Discretionary Trusts

The IHT rules for discretionary trusts now also apply to most lifetime interest in possession trusts created on or after 22 March 2006.

There are three elements:

Creation of the Trust

- This will be a chargeable lifetime transfer with tax payable at 20% if it takes the settlor's cumulative total over the nil-rate band.
- If the settlor dies within seven years, there may be further tax to pay. If this is between three and seven years, taper relief may apply.

Periodic charges (also known as the principle charge)

- Apply to the trust, not the settlor.
- Will apply whether or not the settlor is alive or dead.
- This will occur on every ten-year anniversary of the trust creation.
- The charge is 30% of the current lifetime rate (presently 20%). This makes the maximum charge 6% of the value of the trust fund.
- The seven-year IHT cumulation of the settlor immediately before the creation of the trust is taken.
- Any capital distributions within the previous ten years also need to be taken into account.

Exit charge (also known as the proportionate charge)

- This charge applies to capital leaving the trust.
- Taxed at 30% of the effective rate from the start of the trust, or if it is after ten years, the effective rate from the last periodic charge.
- If there was no IHT to pay on creation due to the amount being within the nil-rate band, the effective rate would be nil so there would be no exit charge.
- It is then time apportioned by the number of complete successive quarter years since the last periodic charge (expressed as n/40ths).

EXAMPLE

John made a transfer of £240,000 to a discretionary trust on the 1 October 1999, when the nil-rate band was £234,000. John had made no other gifts prior to setting up the trust. A capital payment of £33,000 was made from the trust to a beneficiary in January 2003.

The value of the trust as at the 1 October 2010 is £405,000.

No charge on creation since two annual exemptions plus the nil-rate band cover the amount.

No exit charge on capital payment since effective rate was nil.

Periodic charge

Value of the trust at 10th anniversary	£405,000
plus capital disbursement of	£ 33,000
Total amount subject to IHT	£438,000
less current nil-rate band	£325,000
leaves taxable amount of	£113,000 tax at 20%: £22,600

Effective rate: £22,600 ÷ £405,000 = 5.58%

Tax charge: £405,000 x 5.58% x 30% = £6,780 (Payable by the trustees from the trust fund)

(Note: alternative method: £113,000 x 6% = £6,780 arrives at the same answer.)

Further example: A further capital payment of £30,000 is made from the trust to a beneficiary on the 21 March 2012.

Exit charge

30% of the effective rate from last 10th anniversary: 5.58 x 30% = 1.674%

£30,000 capital distributed on 21 March 2011 £30,000 x 1.674% = £502.20

Time apportionment: 1/10/10 to 21/03/12 = 1 year 3+ months = 5 quarter years = 5/40

£502.20 x 5/40 = £62.78 payable by the recipient.

5.3.4   Trusts for Minors

Rules were introduced by the Finance Act 2006 to cater for two types of trust created by the death of a parent. These allow the accumulation of income but do not incur the full application of the periodic or exit charge rules.

Trusts for bereaved minors

- May be created on the death of a parent (by will or on intestacy) or under the Criminal Injuries Compensation Scheme.
- Must provide an absolute interest at 18.
- Until then, trust treated as child's for IHT purposes (like pre 2006 interest in possession trusts).
- No periodic charge or exit charge at 18.

18 to 25 Trusts

- May be created on the death of a parent (by will or on intestacy) or under the Criminal Injuries Compensation Scheme.
- Must provide an absolute entitlement by the age of 25.
- Trust treated as child's for IHT purposes until 18.
- Exit charge payable on absolute entitlement based on the period since the beneficiary's 18th birthday.

AIMS

The aims of this paper are to:

1. Develop a broad understanding of the principles of private client investment within the context of the current regulatory environment.

2. Identify the investment requirements of clients from the relevant information available.

3. Select suitable products available to meet the clients' needs.

4. Demonstrate the ability to communicate conclusions to a client in an appropriate manner.

5. Ensure that students develop the skills to maintain their competence and knowledge.

ASSESSMENT STRUCTURE

A 3-hour paper divided into three sections:

SECTION A: Ten compulsory short answer questions. This section will carry 40% of the marks.

SECTION B: Three essays of which students will be expected to answer one. In this section, students are expected to show depth of knowledge on a particular topic and be able to discuss all aspects of the subject in question. This section will carry 20% of the marks.

SECTION C: One compulsory structured question comprising a number of parts, based on a case study in which the students' ability to give investment advice will be tested. This section will carry 40% of the marks.

Tax tables, RPI figures and Market Makers' Gilts lists will be provided.

READING LIST

At the end of this syllabus we have supplied a reading list. Candidates attempting this examination are strongly advised to relate their reading to practitioner experience. Candidates who read more widely and can draw on this broader context fare better in higher, post graduate level examinations of this nature, where both breadth and depth are required.

SECTION ONE

FINANCIAL ADVICE WITHIN A REGULATED ENVIRONMENT

Learning Outcome:

Candidates will be able to assess the implications of the UK legal and regulatory framework as they apply to the provision of private client investment advice.

Assessment Criteria:

Candidates can:

- Interpret the regulatory environment, supervision and rules governing private client advice and management in the UK

- Summarise the fiduciary responsibility towards customers and their legal right to recourse

- Assess the regulatory requirements of the main investment trading and settlement mechanisms within the UK and overseas

- Determine how the factors above govern and influence the business processes and practice of private client advice and management

Learning Objectives:

1. The Legal and Regulatory Framework

1. Understand the main provisions of the FSMA 2000 and associated Secondary Legislation and assess their implications for the business operations of the private client adviser.

2. Understand the aims of the European Financial Services Action Plan, and evaluate the effects of MiFID and CRD on the business systems and controls of the private client adviser.

3. Understand the role, regulatory objectives and functions of the Financial Conduct Authority (FCA) and Prudential Regulation Authority (PRA) and how they affect the control structures of firms.

4. Relate the FCA's Principles and Conduct of Business rules to the processes of advising clients, managing investments, and reporting to customers.

5. Apply the rules on 'treating customers fairly' and 'client's best interest' to the process of advising clients.

6. Know the extent of an investment adviser's duty to disclose material information about a recommended investment.

7. Identify 'conflicts of interest' and their potential impact on clients and business operations, and understand the compliance requirements that exist to prevent such occurrences.

8. Understand the fiduciary responsibilities of intermediaries, the rights of aggrieved customers and the rules for handling complaints.

9. Understand the principal measures to combat financial crime (Insider dealing, Market Abuse, Money Laundering) and evaluate their impact on the firm, the private client adviser and the process of advising and managing private client investments

SECTION TWO

INVESTMENT TAXATION

Learning Outcome:

Candidates will be able to assess the impact of taxation on the evaluation of investments and the provision of investment advice.

Assessment Criteria:

Candidates can:

- Summarise the basic structure of the UK tax system

- Determine the impact of the main taxes (on income and capital) that may be charged to individuals

- Determine the impact of domicile and residence on an individual's liability to UK tax

- Assess the impact of taxation on the investment decision-making process, and the need to tailor an appropriate strategy according to the needs of the client and the range of strategies available

NOTE: All references to taxation refer to taxes applicable in the United Kingdom; tax tables will be provided in the examination where necessary.

Learning Objectives:

A. Income Tax

1. Understand the role of HMRC and the structure of the UK self-assessment tax system.

2. Understand when and how income tax is applied to earnings, interest and dividends and, in some cases, capital gains.

3. Be able to calculate simple tax computations.

4. Apply the main rules relating to allowable deductions, personal allowances and reliefs, marriage and civil partnerships and their breakdown, and the tax liabilities of minors.

5. Understand the tax treatment of different kinds of investments and the taxation of income arising on overseas investments.

6. Evaluate the tax efficiency of an investment asset within the wider context of suitability for an individual customer.

B. Capital Gains Tax

7. Understand the principles of Capital Gains Tax, and when and how it arises.

8. Understand the main CGT exemptions and reliefs available including main residence, exempt assets and exemption limits applicable for individuals, trusts and estates.

9. Understand the main disposal rules for CGT, including special rules that apply to disposals on death and between spouses/ civil partners.

10. Know the calculations applicable to assets purchased prior to and post–31 March 1982.

11. Be able to calculate taxable gains on an individual's net gains for a fiscal year.

12. Understand due dates for paying CGT and the use of CGT deferral.

C. Inheritance Tax

13. Understand the liability to IHT, and the effects on IHT liability of chargeable lifetime transfers and transfers on death.

14. Understand IHT exemptions and reliefs, excluded assets, Potentially Exempt Transfers, and gifts with reservation.

15. Understand the rules governing the administration of estates, grant of probate and registration of probate.

16. Be able to value assets for probate and life time transfers.

17. Be able to calculate IHT liability based on a straightforward example.

18. Understand the relationship between the valuation of assets for CGT purposes, and valuation of assets for IHT-related chargeable lifetime and estate transfers.

D. Offshore Tax

19. Understand the tax treatment of on shore and off shore funds.

20. Evaluate the suitability of an offshore investment for a UK-domiciled individual.

SECTION THREE

FINANCIAL MARKETS

Learning Outcome:

Candidates will be able to evaluate the relevance of market-related factors that can influence investment decisions, processes and advice.

Assessment Criteria:

Candidates can:

- Differentiate between the key features of the main UK and overseas markets (including fixed income and equity) and specify the purpose and methods of trading, settlement, registration and holding of assets

- Assess and justify the political, economic and practical risks, costs and benefits of trading or investing in a particular market

- Assess the suitability and appropriateness of trading or investing in certain markets to help meet the investment objectives of a private customer

- Explain the purposes of and requirements issuing contract notes and the operation of nominee companies

Learning Objectives:

A. World Financial Markets

1. Understand the relative size of world equity markets and predominant asset sectors within each market.

2. Know the key features of the global government and corporate bond markets.

3. Understand the relative benefits, risks and costs of investing in developed and emerging markets.

4. Understand and differentiate between exchange-traded, over-the-counter and alternative markets.

5. Apply the principles of asset and liability matching when managing investments in different currencies.

6. Understand how indices are constructed, and the purposes and limitations in using them.

B. UK Markets

7. Understand the main organisations and processes for transacting, clearing, settling and safekeeping domestic financial securities.

8. Know the methods by which domestic securities are issued and brought to market.

9. Be aware of the purposes and requirements for issuing contract notes.

10. Understand the applicability of VAT, Stamp Duty and Stamp Duty Reserve Tax to transactions in financial securities.

11. Understand the purposes and operation of nominee companies.

SECTION FOUR

TRUSTS AND TRUSTEES

Learning Outcome:

Candidates will be able to understand the principles and key features of Trusts and the law governing their creation and management.

Assessment Criteria:

- Compare the main types of Trusts available under UK law, their key features and taxation considerations

- Explain the benefits, limitations and requirements to achieve Charitable Status

- Evaluate the taxation implications of different scenarios involving Trusts

- Evaluate the merits of using a Trust as a means to achieve a specific client objective

Learning Objectives:

A. Trusts and Trust Legislation

1. Know the key features of Trusts – arrangement, participants, types, documentation.

2. Know the different types of Trust and what each is designed to achieve.

3. Understand the key provisions of the Trustee Act 2000 and how these relate to the investment powers of Trustees and the Trust Deed.

B. Taxation of Trusts

4. Understand the concept of a Chargeable Lifetime Transfer and be able to assess the IHT consequences of different scenarios relating to interest in possession.

5. Know the requirements for Charitable status, how Charities are taxed, and the purpose and rules of Gift Aid.

CISI Membership

Studying for a CISI qualification is hard work and we're sure you're putting in plenty of hours, but don't lose sight of your goal! This is just the first step in your career; there is much more to achieve!

The securities and investments industry attracts ambitious and driven individuals. You're probably one yourself and that's great, but on the other hand you're almost certainly surrounded by lots of other people with similar ambitions. So how can you stay one step ahead during these uncertain times?

Entry Criteria:

Pass in either:

- Investment Operations Certificate (IOC), IFQ, ICWM, CISI Certificates in, eg, Securities, Derivatives or Investment Management, Advanced Certificates
- One or two CISI Diploma/Masters Papers

Joining Fee:

£25 or free if applying via prefilled application form

Annual Subscription (pro rata): £125

Using your new CISI qualification* to become an Associate (ACSI) member of the Chartered Institute for Securities & Investment could well be the next important career move you make this year, and help you maintain your competence.

Join our global network of over 50,000 financial services professionals and start enjoying both the professional and personal benefits that CISI membership offers. Once you become a member you can use the prestigious ACSI designation after your name and even work towards becoming personally chartered.

* ie, Investment Operations Certificate (IOC), IFQ, CISI Certificate Programme

Turn over to find out more about CISI membership

" ...competence is not just about examinations. It is about skills, knowledge, expertise, ethical behaviour and the application and maintenance of all these.

April 2008
FSA, Retail Distribution Review Interim Report

Becoming an Associate member of CISI offers you...

• Use of the CISI CPD Scheme

• Unlimited free CPD seminars

• Highly recognised designatory letters

• Free access to online training tools including Professional Refresher and Infolink

• Free webcasts and podcasts

• Unlimited free attendance at CISI Professional Forums

• CISI publications including *S&I Review* and *Change – The Regulatory Update*

• 20% discount on all CISI conferences and training courses

• Invitation to CISI Annual Lecture

• Select Benefits – our exclusive personal benefits portfolio

Plus many other networking opportunities which could be invaluable for your career.

To upgrade your student membership to Associate,

get in touch...

+44 20 7645 0777
customersupport@cisi.org
cisi.org/membership

CISI

CHARTERED INSTITUTE FOR
SECURITIES & INVESTMENT

CISI Elearning Products
Revision Express Interactive

You've bought the workbook...
...now test your knowledge before your exam.

CISI elearning products are high-quality, interactive and engaging learning tools and revision aids which can be used in conjunction with CISI workbooks (IOC, Certificate, Investment Advice Diploma, PCIAM, and certain international titles), or to help you remain up-to-date with regulatory developments in order to meet compliance requirements.

Features of CISI elearning products include:

• Questions throughout to reaffirm understanding of the subject
• All modules now contain questions that reflect as closely as possible the standard you will experience in your examination*
• Interactive exercises and tutorials

* (please note, however, they are not the CISI examination questions themselves)

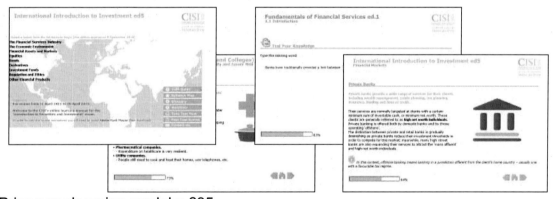

Price per elearning module: £35
Price when purchased with the CISI workbook: £100 (normal price: £110)

Professional Refresher

Self-testing elearning modules to refresh your knowledge, meet regulatory and firm requirements, and earn CPD hours.

Professional Refresher is an online learning system which allows self-administered refresher testing on a variety of topics, including the latest regulatory changes. There are currently more than 50 modules available, with new and topical modules being added on a regular basis.

Benefits to firms:
• Learning and tests can form part of a business T&C programme
• Learning and tests kept up to date and accurate by the CISI
• Relevant and useful – devised by industry practitioners
• Access to individual results via a management overview facility
• Cost-effective – no additional charge for CISI members
• Available to non-members

Benefits to individuals:
• Comprehensive selection of topics across industry sectors
• Modules are frequently reviewed and updated by industry experts
• New topics introduced regularly
• Free for members
• Successfully passed modules are recorded in your CPD log as Active learning
• Counts as Structured learning for RDR purposes
• On completion of a module, a certificate can be printed out for your own records

The full suite of Professional Refresher modules is free to CISI members or £150 for non-members. Modules are also available individually.

To view a full list of Professional Refresher modules visit:

cisi.org/refresher

Or for more information call:

+44 20 7645 0670

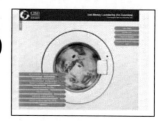

Or email:

crm@cisi.org

Feedback to CISI

Have you found this workbook to be a valuable aid to your studies? We would like your views, so please email us (learningresources@cisi.org) with any thoughts, ideas or comments.

Accredited Training Providers

Support for examination students studying for the Chartered Institute for Securities & Investment (CISI) Qualifications is provided by several Accredited Training Providers (ATPs), including Fitch Learning and BPP. The CISI's ATPs offer a range of face-to-face training courses, distance learning programmes, their own learning resources and study packs which have been accredited by the CISI. The CISI works in close collaboration with its accredited training providers to ensure they are kept informed of changes to CISI examinations so they can build them into their own courses and study packs.

CISI Workbook Specialists Wanted

Workbook Authors

Experienced freelance authors with finance experience, and who have published work in their area of specialism, are sought. Responsibilities include:
• Updating workbooks in line with new syllabuses and any industry developments
• Ensuring that the syllabus is fully covered

Workbook Reviewers

Individuals with a high-level knowledge of the subject area are sought. Responsibilities include:
• Highlighting any inconsistencies against the syllabus
• Assessing the author's interpretation of the workbook

Workbook Technical Reviewers

Technical reviewers provide a detailed review of the workbook and bring the review comments to the panel. Responsibilities include:
• Cross-checking the workbook against the syllabus
• Ensuring sufficient coverage of each learning objective

Workbook Proofreaders

Proofreaders are needed to proof workbooks both grammatically and also in terms of the format and layout. Responsibilities include:
• Checking for spelling and grammar mistakes
• Checking for formatting inconsistencies

If you are interested in becoming a CISI external specialist telephone:

+44 20 7645 0609

Notes

Notes

Notes